The Holy Spirit

Understanding his
work in our lives

by Pete and Anne Woodcock

thegoodbook
COMPANY

The Holy Spirit
Understanding His work in our lives
© Pete and Anne Woodcock/The Good Book Company, 2006. Reprinted 2009, 2010, 2014.
Series Consultants: Tim Chester, Tim Thornborough,
                    Anne Woodcock, Carl Laferton

The Good Book Company
Tel (UK): 0333 123 0880
Tel (US): 866 244 2165
Tel (int): + (44) 208 942 0880
Email: info@thegoodbook.co.uk

Websites
UK: www.thegoodbook.co.uk
North America: www.thegoodbook.com
Australia: www.thegoodbook.com.au
New Zealand: www.thegoodbook.co.nz

Unless indicated, all Scripture references are taken from the HOLY BIBLE, NEW
INTERNATIONAL VERSION. Copyright © 1973, 1978, 1984, 2011 by Biblica, Inc.
Used by permission. All rights reserved worldwide

ISBN: 9781905564217

Printed in the Czech Republic

CONTENTS

introduction: good book guides

Every Bible-study group is different—yours may take place in a church building, in a home or in a cafe, on a train, over a leisurely mid-morning coffee or squashed into a 30-minute lunch break. Your group may include new Christians, mature Christians, non-Christians, mums and tots, students, businessmen or teens. That's why we've designed these *Good Book Guides* to be flexible for use in many different situations.

Our aim in each session is to uncover the meaning of a passage, and see how it fits into the "big picture" of the Bible. But that can never be the end. We also need to appropriately apply what we have discovered to our lives. Let's take a look at what is included:

⊕ **Talkabout:** Most groups need to "break the ice" at the beginning of a session, and here's the question that will do that. It's designed to get people talking around a subject that will be covered in the course of the Bible study.

⊔ **Investigate:** The Bible text for each session is broken up into manageable chunks, with questions that aim to help you understand what the passage is about. **The Leader's Guide** contains **guidance on questions**, and sometimes ⊻ additional "follow-up" questions.

⊡ **Explore more (optional):** These questions will help you connect what you have learned to other parts of the Bible, so you can begin to fit it all together like a jig-saw; or occasionally look at a part of the passage that's not dealt with in detail in the main study.

⊡ **Apply:** As you go through a Bible study, you'll keep coming across **apply** sections. These are questions to get the group discussing what the Bible teaching means in practice for you and your church. ⊡ **Getting personal** is an opportunity for you to think, plan and pray about the changes that you personally may need to make as a result of what you have learned.

⊡ **Pray:** We want to encourage prayer that is rooted in God's word—in line with his concerns, purposes and promises. So each session ends with an opportunity to review the truths and challenges highlighted by the Bible study, and turn them into prayers of request and thanksgiving.

The **Leader's Guide** and introduction provide historical background information, explanations of the Bible texts for each session, ideas for **optional extra** activities, and guidance on how best to help people uncover the truths of God's word.

why study The Holy Spirit?

"Receive the Holy Spirit." (John 20 v 22)

You may have heard a lot about the Holy Spirit… or very little. Are you fascinated by what appears to be on offer from those who claim to have the Spirit? Or confused, and put off by the strange things that the Spirit is supposed to do? There are so many disagreements and divisions around this question of how the Spirit of God works in our lives.

To discover the truth about the Holy Spirit we need to investigate carefully what the Bible says about Him. These eight sessions have been constructed from a survey of every single verse in the Bible that mentions the Holy Spirit. The main themes have been decided by some of the main themes of the Bible's teaching—although eight sessions can't cover everything the Bible teaches about the Spirit. And because so much of what we hear about the Spirit comes to us second or third-hand, we may be in for some surprises!

Two foundational truths about the Spirit are not specifically covered:

• The Holy Spirit is a person, not a force (He is referred to as "He").

• The Holy Spirit is God—the third person of the Trinity (He is referred to as both the Spirit of God and the Spirit of Christ).

In the early days of the Christian church, a sorcerer called Simon offered the apostles money with the words: "Give me also this ability so that everyone on whom I lay my hands may receive the Holy Spirit". For Simon, the Spirit was not a person but a powerful force that he hoped to dispense as he wished; the Spirit was not God but simply a tool to make Simon great; the Spirit was nothing to do with glorifying Jesus Christ, but all about glorifying Simon.

Sadly, it's the same today. Many people who speak about the Spirit are trying to use Him for their own ends, as Simon did. This isn't just getting hold of the wrong end of the stick—Peter called it "wickedness". It's vital then that we know the truth about the Spirit. And more than that, each of us needs to receive Him, not so that we can do great things, but so that God's work may be done in our lives.

1

1 Corinthians 2 v 1-16
THE SPIRIT AND THE BIBLE

⊕ talkabout

1. How is it possible to know about God? Discuss how people often answer this question. How would Christians answer differently?

⊕ investigate

When Paul wrote his first letter to the "problem church" at Corinth, the Christians there were much more taken with worldly philosophies than the apostles' teaching about Jesus Christ. In fact, a quick scan of 1 Corinthians chapter 1 gives the distinct impression that the Corinthians were embarrassed, not only about the message, but also about Paul's chosen method of communicating the message—simply by preaching it. For instance, they were clearly much more interested in the possibility of Paul being a baptiser than a preacher (1 v 13-17).

Paul, however, was clear about his calling, given by Christ Himself, "to preach the gospel—not with [human] wisdom" (v 17). He was completely aware of what others thought of his ministry—"foolishness" (v 18, 21). He was also aware of what people expected in a message from God—"Jews demand [miraculous] signs and Greeks look for wisdom" (v 22). He knew what people were thinking, but he was certainly not going to pander to their expectations; he had utter confidence that preaching Christ crucified is both the power and wisdom of God (v 24), and far greater than any human wisdom or power (v 25). Human nature doesn't change, so we shouldn't be surprised that people today are also disappointed in the "mere" preaching of Christ crucified, and critical of those in Christian work who don't pursue miraculous signs or human wisdom.

Having dealt with false ideas about how to communicate God's message, in 1 Corinthians chapter 2 Paul sets out the true nature of this message, which he calls "the testimony about God" (v 1), "God's wisdom" (v 7), "words taught by the Spirit" (v 13) and "the mind of Christ" (v 16). This is where we will find out how we can know about God!

> **▶ Read 1 Corinthians 2 v 1-16**

2. How does Paul summarise the content of the message (v 2)?

3. Paul has already explained that he is not prepared to use miraculous signs or human wisdom to persuade people (see 1 Corinthians 1 v 22-25). So what is it that makes Paul's message persuasive (v 4-5)?

4. Who is unable to understand the message (v 6, 8, 14)? Why?

5. Who *can* understand the message (v 14-15)? Why?

6. Why do we need the Spirit to understand God's message (v 10-11)?

7. In what form does God's message come to us, according to verse 13?

⊡ explore more

Read the following Bible passages. How do they agree with what we
have learned so far?
- 2 Peter 1 v 20-21
- Hebrews 1 v 1-2
- 1 Peter 1 v 10-12

⊡ apply

8.   Is it possible to know God? How?

9.   How should this affect:
- our response to the message about Jesus Christ? (See also John 14
  v 23-24 and Hebrews 2 v 1.)

- our attitude to academics and so-called experts who look down on
  Christian beliefs?

- the way we share God's message with others?

Do you know God's message about Jesus Christ? If not, what can you do about it? Can you accept God's message? If not, what do you need?

⊥ investigate

In Hebrews 1 v 1-2 (see *explore more* section on page 9) we are told that God has spoken to us in two ways: first, through the prophets of old, "at many times and in various ways"—this is the Old Testament. Secondly, "in these last days ... by his Son"—this is contained for us in the New Testament, where the life, teaching and significance of Jesus has been set down in writing by His apostles. The next part of this session looks at the role of the Spirit in God's revelation through the Old and New Testament writings.

10. What was the role of the Spirit in the production of the Old Testament? Look at the following Bible passages and complete the table.

Bible passage	Who's speaking/ writing?	Who is being quoted?	What is said about the Spirit?
Matthew 22 v 43			
Acts 1 v 16		(v 20)	
Acts 28 v 25			
Hebrews 3 v 7		(v 7-11)	
Hebrews 10 v 15		(v 16)	

11. How has God spoken to us in these last days (Hebrews 1 v 2), and what is the role of the Spirit in that? Look at the following Bible passages and complete the table.

Bible passage	Who does the Spirit help?	What does the Spirit do?
John 3 v 31-34		
John 14 v 16-26		

12. So what should our attitude be to the Old Testament?
And what should our attitude be to the New Testament?

▶ Read 2 Timothy 3 v 16-17

13. How does this passage agree with what we have learned so far about how God reveals Himself?

• Look at verse 16. What do you think "God-breathed" means?

• Look at verse 17. What can the Scripture do for us? So do we need more revelation from God?

⊡ apply

14. Summarise what you have learned about the Spirit and the Bible.

• How do people carve up the Bible into parts that are trustworthy or relevant, and parts that are not? Why is that wrong?

• How do Christians sometimes separate the Spirit from God's word, the Bible? Why is that wrong?

⊡ getting personal

Do you need to change your view of the Bible, the Spirit, or the way in which God speaks today? Ask God to help you make changes in line with what you have learned in this session.

↑ pray

God has spoken to you—and you can know Him! Thank Him for His wonderful grace.

How do you respond to God's word? Ask for God's Spirit to help you accept and obey.

Pray for those who do not understand or accept God's message about Jesus Christ.

Various

2 THE SPIRIT AND THE OLD TESTAMENT

The story so far

God speaks to us in words taught by the Spirit. He is involved both in how God's word was produced, and in us understanding and believing it.

⊕ talkabout

1. It has been said that we must interpret the Old Testament in the light of the New Testament. Give some examples of what happens if we don't follow this advice.

↓ investigate

The Holy Spirit is first mentioned at the very beginning of the Old Testament, in Genesis 1 v 2. He is the Creator and Sustainer of all life. If you check out the following verses—Job 33 v 4 and 34 v 14; Psalm 104 v 29-30—you will see that there is no life without the Spirit. If He withdraws, all life collapses. Without Him everything returns to dark, formless emptiness, as it was in the beginning (Genesis 1 v 2). Clearly, it's absolutely vital that God gives His Spirit.

This session will look at how God has done that throughout Bible history—first, how did He give His Spirit in the Old Testament, and secondly, what was promised in the Old Testament about how God planned to give the Spirit in New Testament times? In order to answer these questions, this session has been constructed as a survey of many Old and New Testament references.

OLD TESTAMENT SPIRIT INDIVIDUALS

2. Look up the following verses and answer the questions given in the table.

In the time of Moses	Who had the Spirit?	What did they do?
a. Exodus 31 v 1-7		
b. Numbers 11 v 16-17		
c. Deuteronomy 34 v 9 (see NIV footnote)		
In the time of the judges		
d. Judges 3 v 7-11		
e. Judges 15 v 11-15		
In the time of the kings		
f. 1 Samuel 10 v 1, 6, 9-11		
g. 1 Samuel 16 v 13		
h. 2 Samuel 23 v 1-2		
i. 1 Chronicles 29 v 11-12		
In the time of the prophets		
j. 2 Chronicles 24 v 20		
k. Ezekiel 2 v 1-8		
l. Zechariah 7 v 12		
m. Luke 1 v 67		

3. What three types of activity were carried out by those who were given the Spirit in the Old Testament?

> **Read Numbers 11 v 29**

In this passage God has just given His Spirit to 70 elders of Israel to assist Moses in leading God's people. Joshua however, doesn't really understand and wants to safeguard Moses' unique leadership position. This leads him to protest about two elders who are prophesying outside the tabernacle.

4. Look at Moses' response to Joshua. How does this answer the question of who received God's Spirit in the Old Testament? What does Moses' heartfelt wish tell us?

> **Read 1 Samuel 16 v 14**

5. What does this verse tell us about the gift of the Spirit in the Old Testament (see also Psalm 51 v 11)?

OLD TESTAMENT SPIRIT PROMISES

Moses' hope, in Numbers 11 v 29, is turned into a promise, mostly seen in the Old Testament books of Isaiah and Ezekiel.

A. A promised "Spirit Person"

6. Look up the following verses and answer the questions given in the table.

Bible passage	How is the Spirit-filled person described?	What will the Spirit-filled person do?
Isaiah 11 v 1-5		
Isaiah 42 v 1-4		
Isaiah 61 v 1-3		

B. Promised "Spirit people"

7. Look up the following verses and answer the questions given in the table.

Bible passage	Who is the Spirit given to?	What will the Spirit do?
Ezekiel 36 v 24-27		
Ezekiel 37 v 1-14		
Ezekiel 39 v 25-29		
Joel 2 v 28-32		

THE PROMISES FULFILLED

In this next section we will look at New Testament verses which show the fulfilment of the Old Testament promises about the Spirit.

A. WHO IS THE PROMISED "SPIRIT PERSON"?

8. Look at the following verses and answer the questions given in the table.

Bible passage	Who is the promised Spirit person?	What does He do?
Luke 3 v 16-17		
Luke 3 v 21-22		
Luke 4 v 16-21		
Acts 1 v 4-5		
Acts 2 v 32-33		
Acts 2 v 38-39		

B. WHO ARE THE PROMISED "SPIRIT PEOPLE"?

▶ Read 1 Corinthians 12 v 13; Romans 8 v 9; Titus 3 v 4-7

9. Who are the promised Spirit people and how are the Old Testament promises about them fulfilled? (Use the table in question 7 above to remind yourself of the Old Testament promises.)

10. How does the Spirit come to the promised Spirit people?

> ❭ **Read John 3 v 3-16**

11. How does Jesus use the themes from Ezekiel (see Question Seven above) to show that being a Christian is much more than a matter of intellectual religious belief (v 3-8)?

12. Look at the following verses (v 9-16). How does Jesus relate this work of the Spirit to His own work?

⤷ **apply**

13. How would you respond to someone who seeks to live by the teachings of Jesus, and has deep respect for Him as a great teacher and prophet, but knows nothing about the Holy Spirit?

- Comment on this statment: "I see the Spirit as a divine inspiration that allows me to express myself creatively in art and music, through which I can glorify God."

- Comment on this statement: "I went to a three-hour Holy Spirit meeting where many strange things happened, but Jesus wasn't mentioned."

⊡ getting personal

If you are a Christian, how will you respond to the truth that the Spirit of God lives in you? If you do not have the Spirit, what do you need to do?

⊕ pray

- Thank God for the Lord Jesus Christ, the promised Spirit King and Servant of God, who baptises His people with the Spirit.

- If you are a Christian, ask God to help you, by His Spirit, to live as someone who has been cleansed from all impurity and born again.

- Pray for people who are confused or have been misled about the true work of God's Spirit, who continue to seek for the Spirit, instead of understanding that He already lives in all who are in Christ.

3

Acts 2 v 1-41

BAPTISED WITH THE SPIRIT

The story so far

God speaks to us in words taught by the Spirit. He is involved both in how God's word was produced, and in us understanding and believing it.

The Old Testament promised both a single "Spirit person", and many "Spirit people": this was fulfilled in Jesus, and in His church..

⊕ talkabout

1. Give examples of words or phrases that have completely different meanings when used by different generations or social groups.

⊎ investigate

This next part of this course (Sessions 3 to 7) looks at some of the most common terms that are used about the Spirit in the Bible. You will often find that people use a phrase from the Bible differently from the way in which the Bible uses it. If we hear that phrase used wrongly, when we read it in the Bible, instead of looking at what the Bible actually says, we can read into the passage what we already (wrongly) understand the phrase to mean—that's how easily we can come to a wrong interpretation. That's why it's so important to discover precisely what the Bible means when it uses a particular term. "Baptism with the Spirit" is one of those terms that is often wrongly used, easily misunderstood and needs careful investigation.

There are only seven verses in the New Testament that mention "baptism with (or by) the Spirit". Four of these—Matthew 3 v 11, Mark 1 v 8, Luke 3 v 16 and John 1 v 33—announce that Jesus is the one who will baptise with the Holy Spirit. As we saw in the last session, He is the promised

"Spirit Person", but He is also the one who will give the Spirit to the promised "Spirit people"—the church.

The three remaining verses—Acts 1 v 5, Acts 11 v 16 and 1 Corinthians 12 v 13—will be investigated during this session.

❯ Read Acts 1 v 5 and 11 v 15-17

(In Acts 11 Peter explains to the other apostles how the first non-Jews, from the household of Cornelius, had come to faith in Christ.)

2. What do these two verses tell us about *when* the baptism with the Holy Spirit promised by Jesus took place?

• Acts 1 v 5

• Acts 11 v 15-17

3. Scan the chapters of Acts, between 1 v 5 and 11 v 15-17 to find out precisely when this event took place.

Before we look at the events of the day of Pentecost in detail, we need to understand the difference between an event and its interpretation. An account of an *event* simply describes what happens—see Acts 2 v 1-13 and 41 for a description of the baptism with the Spirit on the day of Pentecost. The interpretation, which explains the significance of the event and what it means for us, comes later. If we are given an *interpretation*, we don't need to guess about the meaning of an event. In fact, we would be wrong to try and come up with our own interpretation; we need to investigate the Bible's interpretation to correctly understand what happened. In Acts 2 v 14-39 we will find Peter's explanation of what was happening, and this is what we must look at to find out what the events of Pentecost were all about, and therefore, within that, what baptism with the Spirit is.

❯ Read Acts 2 v 1-13, 41: The Event

4.   List everything that happened.

5.   What did people at the time understand to be the meaning of the events that they had witnessed (see v 12-13)?

❯ Read Acts 2 v 14-21: The Interpretation (Part I)

6.   How do the events of the day of Pentecost fulfil the promises, found in Joel 2 v 28-32, that Peter quotes?

7.   Imagine that you were in the crowd that witnessed these events. What might you expect people to talk about? (See Acts 2 v 7-8.)

❯ Read Acts 2 v 22-37: The Interpretation (Part II)

8.   What does Peter talk about? List the main points in his sermon.

9. What event, according to Peter, shows that Jesus is now alive and exalted in heaven, even though the audience cannot see Him?

> **Read Acts 2 v 37-40: The Interpretation (Part III)**

10. Why were the people cut to the heart?

11. Why was Peter's message good news?

12. What is promised in verses 38-39? Who is this for?

13. What do the events of the day of Pentecost show us about the work of the Spirit…

• in regard to Jesus?

• in regard to the apostles?

• in regard to the audience?

❯ **Read 1 Corinthians 12 v 13**

14. After the day of Pentecost, who is baptised with the Spirit? And what is the effect of baptism with the Spirit (see also v 3)?

• From what we have read in this study, write a short summary of what the baptism of the Spirit actually is.

➔ apply

15. What would you expect to see in someone who claims to have been baptised with the Spirit?

• "No one can say, 'Jesus is Lord,' except by the Holy Spirit" (1 Corinthians 12 v 3). Why not?

⊡ getting personal

If you are a Christian, do you understand that you have been baptised with the Holy Spirit? If the truths taught in this session are new to you, in what ways do you need to change?

⬆ pray

- Thank God that Jesus Christ, the loving Saviour of the world, is the one who has been enthroned at God's right hand.

- Ask God to help you live and speak boldly for Jesus, who is your Lord and Christ.

- Pray for your church and leaders, that your Christian ministry to the local community may be used by the Spirit to bring many to Christ.

4 THE GIFT OF THE SPIRIT

The story so far

God speaks to us in words taught by the Spirit. He is involved both in how God's word was produced, and in us understanding and believing it.

The Old Testament promised both a single "Spirit person", and many "Spirit people": this was fulfilled in Jesus, and in His church.

The first baptism of the Spirit took place at Pentecost, a unique event. Since then, baptism with the Spirit = becoming a Christian.

⊕ talkabout

1. What do most people think when they hear the term "born-again Christian"? What about you?

⊕ investigate

In Acts 2 v 38 Peter talks about "the gift of the Holy Spirit". In the last session we saw that what Peter was speaking of in this verse could also be referred to as "baptism with the Spirit" (compare what happened in Acts 2 v 38 with what is explained in 1 Corinthians 12 v 13). But is it always true that "baptism with the Spirit" = "the gift of the Spirit?" That is the question that this session aims to answer.

The heading for this session is "The gift of the Spirit". However, there are a number of terms that are used for the giving of the Spirit.

2. Look up the following verses and answer the questions given in the table.

Acts...	What words describe the giving of the Spirit?	Who is the Spirit given to?	What led to this?	Are there any other events connected with this?
1 v 4-5				
1 v 8				
2 v 4				
2 v 33				v 33-36
2 v 38			v 37	v 41
8 v 15			v 12	v 15,17
8 v 16				
8 v 17				
9 v 17			v 4-6, 17	v 18
10 v 44				
10 v 45				
10 v 47				
11 v 15				v 18
11 v 16				
11 v 17				
15 v 8				v 9
19 v 6		v 1-5	v 2	

3. What do you notice about the words used for the giving of the Spirit?

4. In each incident…
- what happens before the gift of the Spirit (apart from the first three references in the table)?

- what is always the response from others?

5. Which features only occur sometimes? What does this tell us?

⮕ apply

6. If someone says to you that you can't have received the Spirit because you don't speak in tongues, or because no one has laid hands on you, how would you respond?

⊍ **investigate**

7. From the verses that we have looked at in Acts, is it correct to say that receiving the gift of the Spirit = becoming a Christian?

What we have found in Acts is a description of events. However, we need to remember that a description is not the same as an explanation. We need to read other parts of the New Testament—Gospels and letters—for a fuller explanation of these events.

▶ **Read Titus 3 v 4-7**

8. What is being explained in these verses?

9. What is similar to the passages from Acts?

10. What else do we learn about what the Holy Spirit does for us?
Write down all the benefits of receiving the gift of the Spirit—and take
time to appreciate how wonderful God's gift to us is.

➔ apply

11. With these themes in mind, what would you say to someone who thinks
that Christianity is a rather boring religion of "dos and don'ts"?

- How would you respond to someone who, while accepting that you are
  a Christian, also tells you that you have not yet received the Spirit, and
  who claims to be able to give you the Spirit?

⤓ investigate

> **❯ Read John 3 v 1-16**

12. How do these words of Jesus fit with what we have read in Acts?

⊡ apply

13. Why are the following statements inadequate or wrong?

"I am a Christian because…

• I have been baptised."

• someone laid hands on me and I spoke in tongues."

• I believe that Jesus is the Son of God."

⊡ getting personal

Has this session changed your view of what a Christian is?
Can you rejoice that you have received the gift of the Spirit in your life?

⊡ pray

Look again at Titus 3 v 4-7. Use this passage to help you…
• praise and thank God.
• confess any sins.
• ask for help in living as a true Christian.

5

Romans 8 v 12-17; Galatians 5 v 16-26

LED BY THE SPIRIT

The story so far

God speaks to us in words taught by the Spirit. The Old Testament promised both a single "Spirit person", and many "Spirit people": this was fulfilled in Jesus, and in His church.

The first baptism of the Spirit took place at Pentecost, a unique event. Since then, baptism with the Spirit = becoming a Christian.

The gift of the Spirit = baptism with the Spirit = becoming a Christian.

⊕ talkabout

1. What do people usually mean when they say that they have been "led by the Spirit" or "led by God"? What is the difference between a strong desire and God's "leading"?

⊕ investigate

As in the last session, we need to find out exactly how the term "led by the Spirit" is used in the Bible. Otherwise we will impose our own definition and end up reading the Bible wrongly.

There are only four references to being led by the Spirit in the Bible, and all of them are found in the New Testament. As we will see later, two of these verses are about Jesus and two are about Christians.

"LED BY GOD" IN THE OLD TESTAMENT

Note: Although the word "God" rather than "Spirit" is used in these verses, this survey gives a biblical backdrop to the subject of being led by the Spirit in the New Testament.

2. Look up the following verses and answer the questions given in the table.

Bible passage	Who was leading?	Who was being led?	Where were they being led?
Exodus 13 v 17-18			
Psalm 106 v 9			
Ezekiel 20 v 10			
Deut. 8 v 2, 15			
Neh. 9 v 12			
Judges 2 v 1			

⊟ apply

3. If an Old Testament Israelite in the desert had said: "I feel God is leading me to go back to Egypt and start a melon farm", how would you have answered him?

⊡ investigate

JESUS "LED BY THE SPIRIT"

> **Read Luke 4 v 1-13 (see also Matthew 4 v 1-11; Mark 1 v 12-13)**

4. What similarities are there with the exodus? What differences are there (compare Hebrews 3 v 7-8 and 4 v 15)?

5. Where did the Spirit lead Jesus? Why?

CHRISTIANS "LED BY THE SPIRIT"

> **Read Romans 8 v 12-17; Galatians 5 v 16-26**

Note: The NIV translation of Galatians 5 v 16 and 25 is confusing because it uses the word "live" to mean two separate things:

a. verse 16: "live" = "be obedient to what the Spirit wants" (translated in other versions as "walk by the Spirit") ie: *So I say, be obedient to the Spirit and you will not gratify the desires of the flesh.*

b. verse 25: "live" = "born again", "saved" ie: *Since we have been born again by the Spirit, let us keep in step with (be obedient to) the Spirit.*

It would be helpful to read Galatians 5 v 16 and 25 in a more accurate version such as the ESV.

6. Both of these passages show us two ways to live. In the table below list everything that you learn from these verses about the two ways to live.

Flesh (sinful nature)	Spirit
Romans 8 v 12-17	Romans 8 v 12-17
Galatians 5 v 16-26	Galatians 5 v 16-26

7. Look at both passages. Who is being led by the Spirit?

8. Look at Romans 8 v 12-17. Where are these people led *to?*
- • v 13

- • v 13

- • v 14

- • v 17

- • v 17

9. What does it mean to be "led by the Spirit"?

⊡ apply

10. From what we have learned about being led by the Spirit, what should we expect the Christian life to be like?

- • How could you help a Christian who says: "I'm not doing very well. The Christian life is such a struggle for me. I'm always battling with a particular sin."

⬇ investigate

11. Look at Galatians 5 v 25. What command is given to those who are born again ("live"—NIV) by the Spirit? What does that mean?

12. How does Galatians 5 v 17 describe the reality of what it means to keep in step with the Spirit? Compare this with what we have learned from Romans 8 and the experience of Jesus when He was led by the Spirit.

13. Why is walking such a good picture for living the Christian life?

➔ apply

14. Can you be a Christian, but not be led by the Spirit?

• Can you be a Christian, but not walk by the Spirit?

⊡ getting personal

Have you realised that the Christian life in this world is not one of
comfort and ease, but of struggle and hardship?
In which areas of your life do you need to do battle with your sinful
nature? How will you do this?

↑ pray

- Praise God for Jesus, who has been tempted in every way, just as we
  are, yet was without sin.

- Do you need to confess to your heavenly Father times when you have
  given in to the sinful nature?

- How much of the fruit of the Spirit (Galatians 5 v 22-23) can be seen
  in your life? Ask God to grow and use this fruit for the blessing of
  everyone.

6 Ephesians 5 v 15-22

FILLED WITH THE SPIRIT

The story so far

God speaks to us in words taught by the Spirit.

The first baptism of the Spirit took place at Pentecost, a unique event. Since then, baptism with the Spirit = becoming a Christian.

The gift of the Spirit = baptism with the Spirit = becoming a Christian.

To be led by the Spirit means to be enabled to live the Christian life, battling sin in this world as we struggle on towards a glorious eternal future.

⊕ talkabout

1. Have you ever been drunk? How does drunkenness transform a person?

⊥ investigate

> **Read Ephesians 5 v 15-22**

2. Scan the whole of Ephesians 5. What is the main theme of this passage?

3. Fill in the blanks. Two commands (v 18):

Don't…

Do…

The reason (v 16)…

Therefore (v 17)…

And (v 18)…

4. What are the four actions that show someone is filled with the Spirit (v 19-21)?

-
-
-
-

Note: In the NIV it appears that being filled with the Spirit is the first of several commands that also include speaking to one another, singing and giving thanks to God, and submitting to one another. However, other versions, such as the ESV, more accurately translate all of this as one sentence.

"Be filled with the Spirit, addressing one another in psalms and hymns and spiritual songs, singing and making melody to the Lord with your heart, giving thanks always and for everything to God the Father in the name of our Lord Jesus Christ, submitting to one another out of reverence for Christ."   Ephesians 5 v 18-21 (ESV)

Now we can see that being filled with the Spirit actually is speaking to one another, singing and giving thanks to God and submitting to one another. If you are filled with the Spirit, you do these things—if you're not, you don't.

5. What do these four things have in common?

• Why does Paul call them "being filled with the Spirit", do you think?

6. Would it be correct to describe being filled with the Spirit as an experience? Why or why not?

7. According to the passage, how is getting drunk on wine different to being filled with the Spirit?

8. How is getting drunk on wine similar to being filled with the Spirit? What is the point of the comparison?

> **Read Colossians 3 v 16-17**

This passage, also written by Paul, is a parallel to Ephesians 5 v 18-21. It doesn't mention being filled with the Spirit.

9. What does it mention instead? What conclusions can we draw from this?

⟴ apply

10. How can we tell whether someone is truly filled with the Spirit?

• Notice that Ephesians 5 v 18 gives us a command. How can we obey it?

⊡ **investigate**

11. Look up the following verses and answer the questions given in the table.

Bible passage	Who is filled with the Spirit?	For what purpose?
Luke 1 v 15		v 16-17
Luke 1 v 41		v 42-45
Luke 1 v 67		v 68-69
Acts 2 v 4		v 4, 11
Acts 4 v 8		v 8-12
Acts 4 v 31		
Acts 9 v 17		v 15
Acts 13 v 9		v 10-11
Acts 13 v 52		v 49-51

12. What is the difference between the way in which Luke uses the term "filled with the Spirit", and the way Paul uses it in Ephesians 5?

• Complete the following sentences: In Luke's writing, in contrast to Paul's, being filled with the Spirit is not…

It is …

⤷ apply

13. What would you expect to see in someone who is filled with the Spirit, according to Luke's use of the term?

• How should this encourage us in the task of evangelism?

⌣ getting personal

How are you involved in the church's task of proclaiming the good news about Jesus? How do you feel about doing that—unprepared, unskilled, afraid? How has this session encouraged you?

⤓ pray

- Give thanks to God for those in your church who are filled with the Spirit. Why not name them?

- We often fail to teach one another God's truth, lose our joy in Christ, neglect to give thanks to God, and resist submitting to one another? Ask God to forgive you for the times when you have chosen not to be filled with the Spirit.

- Do you trust that God will empower you by His Spirit to proclaim His message faithfully and boldly, no matter how difficult the situation? Ask Him to help you do that.

1 Corinthians 12 v 4-31
GIFTS OF THE SPIRIT

The story so far

The gift of the Spirit = baptism with the Spirit = becoming a Christian.

To be led by the Spirit means to be enabled to live the Christian life, battling sin in this world as we struggle on towards a glorious eternal future.

To be filled with the Spirit has different meanings, depending on the New Testament writer. It means living the Christian life as part of the church (Paul); or being empowered to prophesy, preach and witness (Luke).

⊕ talkabout

1. Think of ways in which Christians are encouraged/advised to discover the gift that each of them has. What is good or bad about these methods?

⊕ investigate

There are five lists of gifts of the Spirit in the New Testament. They are found in 1 Corinthians 12 v 8-10, 1 Corinthians 12 v 28-30, Romans 12 v 6-8, Ephesians 4 v 11 and 1 Peter 4 v 11. While investigating all these passages, this session will focus particularly on 1 Corinthians 12, looking at the context in which these gifts are given.

2. Look up the verses in the table over the page (all are related to the five lists mentioned above) and note down the word or phrase that is used to describe "gifts of the Spirit".

1 Cor 12 v 4	
1 Cor 12 v 5	
1 Cor 12 v 6	
1 Cor 12 v 7	
1 Cor 12 v 11	
1 Cor 14 v 1	
Romans 12 v 6	
Ephesians 4 v 7	
1 Peter 4 v 10	

- What can we learn about the gifts of the Spirit from the words used to describe them?

3. Write down all the gifts that are mentioned in the five lists.

1 Corinthians 12 v 8-10	
1 Corinthians 12 v 28-30	
Romans 12 v 6-8	
Ephesians 4 v 11	
1 Peter 4 v 11	

4. What can we learn about gifts of the Spirit from comparing the five lists?

• What proportion of the gifts listed would you describe as miraculous?

• Do you think that the table in Question Three represents a complete list of all gifts of the Spirit? If yes, why are the lists different?

5. What can we learn from Peter's concise list?

> Read 1 Corinthians 12 v 12-26

This passage comes between the two lists of gifts in 1 Corinthians 12, and shows us the context in which they were given.

6. What are the main themes of this passage?

7. In what way are all Christians the same?

8. In what way are Christians different?

9. Why is the body such a wonderful illustration of the church?

10. Do all gifts have the same, or different purposes? What is the purpose of gifts of the Spirit (v 7)?

11. What is the common good? How is the purpose of the gifts described in Ephesians 4 v 12-13 and 1 Peter 4 v 10?

• What does 1 Corinthians 13 v 1-3 add?

⤷ **apply**

12. Look at the following statements and discuss whether they are right or wrong.

• "A gift is not given to me for my good; it is given to the church."

- "I love church because it gives me the opportunity to express myself by using my gift."

- "The church has 15 good piano-players, but I want my turn, because piano-playing is my gift."

- "The church needs someone to put out chairs before the meeting. I'm available and able to do this. Is this my gift?"

- "To discover what my gift is, I'm going to work out what I enjoy and what I'm good at, and offer that to the church."

- "God used me in my previous church in a number of ways. In my new church I'm just offering my help wherever I can."

⊡ getting personal

Look at the kinds of things that unhappy body parts would say, in 1 Corinthians 12 v 15-16 and 21. Is that how you feel? Have you realised that you have a part to play in the body of Christ, and that you have been given a gift by the Spirit? Do you understand what your gift is for? How might your attitude to church, and what you do for church, need to change?

⊡ investigate

❯ **Read 1 Corinthians 12 v 28-31**

13. What are the greater gifts? What do these gifts have in common? What is the role of people who have these gifts (see also Acts 6 v 1-4)?

14. Why are the "greater gifts" greater? Compare 1 Corinthians 14 v 1-5.

15. Look at 1 Corinthians 12 v 31. If Christians all have different gifts, how is it that we should all equally desire the greater gifts? How can we desire the greater gifts?

⊟ **apply**

16. What does a church look like when the Spirit is at work?

⊡ **getting personal**

How are you contributing, and how can you contribute, to the common good in your church?

⬆ **pray**

- Reflect on what it means to be part of God's people. What are the benefits and privileges? Thank God that He has made you part of the body of Christ.

- Are you grateful to God for the gifts that He has given you?—then thank Him now. If you don't know or don't like your gift, ask Him to help you.

- Pray for the greater gifts to be given to your church. And pray about how you can help and support those with these greater gifts.

8 THE SPIRIT AND YOU

The story so far

To be led by the Spirit means to be enabled to live the Christian life, battling sin in this world as we struggle on towards a glorious eternal future.

To be filled with the Spirit has different meanings, depending on the New Testament writer. It means living the Christian life as part of the church (Paul); or being empowered to prophesy, preach and witness (Luke).

The gifts of the Spirit are gifts to the church (rather than to individuals), for the purpose of building up the church; so we're to use our gifts to do this.

⊕ talkabout

1. What sort of things can bring a Christian (someone whose sins have been forgiven because of Jesus) under a sense of condemnation, or fear that God no longer loves them?

⊕ investigate

❯ Read Romans 8 v 1-39

As well as being packed full of fantastic teaching, Romans 8 contains more references to the Spirit than any other chapter in the Bible. However, you will soon notice that this passage is all about the work and achievements of Jesus Christ (v 1-4, 9-11, 17, 29-30, 32-35, 39). This shouldn't surprise us, as we have already seen that the work of the Spirit is to glorify Christ. In fact, a number of the things that we look at in this session have already been investigated in previous Bible studies. This is a great opportunity to review these truths and see what a difference they make for people who are suffering or struggling.

2. What is Paul's big theme in this passage (see verses 1, 33-34 and 38-39)?

3. How has Jesus done what the law of God couldn't do for us? Compare Romans 5 v 6.

4. How do we receive the benefit of what Jesus has done for us (v 1-4)? What is *not* the way to receive it?

5. Paul has already told us that undeserving sinners can be made right with God through what Jesus Christ has done (Romans 3 v 22-24). Why is he again stressing that there is no condemnation for those who are "in Christ"? (See Romans 7 v 14-25; 8 v 10, 18, 22.)

⊡ **getting personal**

Think of the worst thing you have done in your life—the thing about which you feel most guilty or embarrassed. If you are "in Christ", don't allow yourself to be condemned by that thing anymore.

6. How can we know whether we are "in Christ" (8 v 9)?

7. How do we know we have the Spirit?
- v 5
- v 13-14 (See Session Five)
- v 15-16

8. Look again at verses 14-16. What is the difference between the relationship of a slave and his master, and that of a son and his father? Think about the following areas…

	Slave/Master	Son/Father
Why obey?		
What happens when you fail?		
What are your hopes for the future?		
What is most important to you?		

9. What is the future for the children of God (v 17)? What does this mean?

10. What is the contrast in verses 18-27 between now and the future? List what Paul says are the characteristics of each for the Christian.

Now	The future

11. What is the thing that we are missing now, and that we hope for? (See also v 10.) How does this affect us at the moment (v 18, 23 and 26)?

12. What does the Spirit do for us now, and how?

13. What is God's loving purpose for His children (v 28-30)? So what will the Spirit ask God on our behalf when He intercedes for us (v 27)?

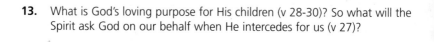 **apply**

14. "We do not know what we ought to pray for." What does this mean? Remember that this is written in the context of suffering (v 18). (Compare Philippians 1 v 21-24.)

- Some people will say that, if God is our Father, we will have perfect health physically and emotionally. How can this teaching bring us under a sense of condemnation again?

- Why is this kind of teaching not only wrong, but in opposition to the work of the Spirit (v 22-25)?

15. What can separate you from the love of God in Christ Jesus?

- If you are "in Christ", what accusation can anyone bring against you?

💬 getting personal

These are wonderful verses. What is the one that really strikes you? How will you use this to set your mind on what the Spirit desires?

⬆ pray

Look again at Romans 8 v 28-39. Use this passage to help you…

- praise and thank God your Father.
- confess and seek forgiveness from God your Father.
- ask for the Spirit's help in living freely, securely and hopefully as an astonishingly loved child of God your Father.

The Holy Spirit: Leader's Guide

INTRODUCTION

Leading a Bible study can be a bit like herding cats—everyone has a different idea of what the passage could be about, and a different line of enquiry that they want to pursue. But a good group leader is more than someone who just referees this kind of discussion. You will want to:

- correctly understand and handle the Bible passage. But also…

- encourage and train the people in your group to do this for themselves. Don't fall into the trap of spoon-feeding people by simply passing on the information in the Leader's Guide. Then…

- make sure that no Bible study is finished without everyone knowing how the passage is relevant for them. What changes do you all need to make in the light of the things you have been learning? And finally…

- encourage the group to turn all that has been learned and discussed into prayer.

Your Bible-study group is unique, and you are likely to know better than anyone the capabilities, backgrounds and circumstances of the people you are leading. That's why we've designed these guides with a number of optional features. If they're a quiet bunch, you might want to spend longer on talkabout. If your time is limited, you can choose to skip explore more, or get people to look at these questions at home. Can't get enough of Bible study? Well, some studies have optional extra homework projects. As leader, you can adapt and select the material to the needs of your particular group.

So what's in the Leader's Guide? The main thing that this Leader's Guide will help you to do is to understand the major teaching points in the passage you are studying, and how to apply them. As well as guidance on the questions, the Leader's Guide for each session contains the following important sections:

THE BIG IDEA

One or two key sentences will give you the main point of the session. This is what you should be aiming to have fixed in people's minds as they leave the Bible study. And it's the point you need to head back towards when the discussion goes off at a tangent.

SUMMARY

An overview of the passage, including plenty of useful historical background information.

OPTIONAL EXTRA

Usually this is an introductory activity that ties in with the main theme of the Bible study, and is designed to "break the ice" at the beginning of a session. Or it may be a "homework project" that people can tackle during the week.

So let's take a look at the various different features of a Good Book Guide:

⊕ talkabout

Each session kicks off with a discussion question, based on the group's opinions or experiences. It's designed to get people talking and thinking in a general way about the main subject of the Bible study.

⊥ investigate

The first thing you and your group need to know is what the Bible passage is about, which is the purpose of these questions. But watch out—people may come up with answers based on their experiences or teaching they have heard in the past, without referring to the passage at all. It's amazing how often we can get through a Bible study without actually looking at the Bible! If you're stuck for an answer, the Leader's Guide contains guidance on questions. These are the answers to direct your group to. This information isn't meant to be read out to people—ideally, you want them to discover these answers from the Bible for themselves. Sometimes there are optional follow-up questions (see ⊻ in guidance on questions) to help you help your group get to the answer.

⊡ explore more

These questions generally point people to other relevant parts of the Bible. They are useful for helping your group to see how the passage fits into the "big picture" of the whole Bible. These sections are OPTIONAL—only use them if you have time. Remember that it's better to finish in good time having really grasped one big thing from the passage, than to try and cram everything in.

→ apply

We want to encourage you to spend more time working at application—too often, it is simply tacked on at the end. In the Good Book Guides, apply sections are mixed in with the investigate sections of the study. We hope that people will realise that application is not just an optional extra, but rather, the whole purpose of studying the

Bible. We do Bible study so that our lives can be changed by what we hear from God's word. If you skip the application, the Bible study hasn't achieved its purpose.

These questions draw out practical lessons that we can all learn from the Bible passage. You can review what has been learned so far, and think about practical differences that this should make in our churches and our lives. The group gets the opportunity to talk about what they personally have learned.

⊡ getting personal

These can be done at home, but it is well worth allowing a few moments of quiet reflection during the study for each person to think and pray about specific changes they need to make in their own lives. Why not have a time for reporting back at the beginning of the following session, so that everyone can be encouraged and challenged by one another to make application a priority?

↑ pray

In Acts 4 v 25-30 the first Christians quoted Psalm 2 as they prayed in response to the persecution of the apostles by the Jewish religious leaders. Today however, it's not as common for Christians to base prayers on the truths of God's word as it once was. As a result, our prayers tend to be weak, superficial and self-centred rather than bold, visionary and God-centred.

The prayer section is based on what has been learned from the Bible passage. How different our prayer times would be if we were genuinely responding to what God has said to us through His word.

1

1 Corinthians 2 v 1-16
THE SPIRIT AND THE BIBLE

THE BIG IDEA

God speaks to us in words taught by the Spirit.

SUMMARY

This session aims to show that the Spirit is fundamentally involved in both producing and receiving God's word. Without the Holy Spirit there is no communication from God to humans. This is vital to understand because many people fall into one of the following two errors.

Some people see the Bible as merely a collection of ancient documents, but the Spirit as an "open channel" to God. This view finds sympathy in our culture, where "spirituality" is highly regarded, while doctrine and dogma are frowned upon. The Bible seems dull and irrelevant to these people, whereas the work of the Spirit seems empowering and exciting. So they tend to ignore the Bible, while at the same time invoking the Spirit a great deal. But without understanding the role of the Spirit as taught in God's word, the way is opened up for all sorts of weird and wacky "manifestations of the Spirit".

Other people, perhaps reacting against the views described above, avoid anything to do with the Spirit. They become scholars and academics of the Bible. But, without a true understanding of the Spirit's role in producing and teaching the Scriptures, why should the Bible be viewed as anything other than an historical source, rather than the life-giving word of God—something to be analysed rather than obeyed? These people are easy prey to liberal ideas that

undermine confidence in the Bible as the authoritative word of God.

This session begins with the foundational question of whether we can know God, and if so, how? The Bible passages investigated seek to establish the following points:

- We can know God only because He has revealed Himself to us.
- God's revelation of Himself is the message of Jesus Christ, His Son, who was crucified.
- The message of Jesus Christ can only be understood and accepted by those who have God's Spirit, since only the Spirit knows the thoughts of God, which are beyond our powers of reason or imagination.
- God's message comes in the form of words—but these are spiritual words taught by the Spirit, and not capable of being grasped by human wisdom.
- Both the Old and New Testaments are equally the words of God, spoken through men by the power of the Holy Spirit, although there are things hidden in the OT that are only revealed in the New.
- Both the teaching of Jesus and the teaching of the apostles are equally the words of God, spoken by the power of the Holy Spirit.
- The written word of God, taught by the power of the Holy Spirit is all that is needed to thoroughly equip us for every good work. The implication is that no further revelation from God is needed after the completion of the Bible.

Note: You may first want to read 1 Corinthians 1 (especially v 17-25) with your group, either aloud or by giving people a few moments to scan the verses, before reading the introduction in the Study Guide. Not only does it reveal something of what was going on at Corinth when Paul wrote his letter, it will also be particularly helpful when discussing what is meant by "a demonstration of the Spirit's power" (2 v 4), in answer to Q3.

GUIDANCE FOR QUESTIONS

1. How is it possible to know about God? Discuss how people often answer this question. Answers may include: through observation and experience (includes empirical investigation); through the use of human reason and/or imagination; through revelation. **How would Christians answer differently?** Christians believe that without revelation—ie: God speaking to us and showing us what He is like—people cannot know anything more than: that there is a God (Romans 1 v 19-20); that we should (although we don't) live up to His requirements (Romans 1 v 32; 2 v 12-15).

2. How does Paul summarise the content of the message (v 2)? "Jesus Christ and him crucified."

3. Paul has already explained that he is not prepared to use miraculous signs or human wisdom to persuade people (see 1 Corinthians 1 v 22-25). So what is it that makes Paul's message persuasive (v 4-5)? The Spirit's power (v 4), which is the same as God's power (v 5).
Note: Some Christians will read v 4 in the following way—Paul's message and preaching came with accompanying miraculous signs ("a demonstration of the Spirit's power") and that's why people were persuaded to come to faith. However, in chapter 1 v 21-23, Paul has already made it clear that he rejects demands for miraculous

signs to authenticate the message from God, and that it is simply through "the foolishness of what was preached" that God saves people. So in this passage, the "demonstration of the Spirit's power" (2 v 4) can't be miraculous signs; rather, it is spiritual understanding (v 12). Elsewhere, the Bible speaks of this as new birth (John 3 v 3-7; Titus 3 v 5). In other words, the Spirit's power is demonstrated when people understand the message that is preached, responding in obedience, and so are saved. It is interesting to note that although the book of Acts does record many occasions when the preaching of the apostles was accompanied by miraculous signs, as time goes on, references to these miraculous signs become less frequent. For instance, accounts of Paul and his co-workers preaching that don't refer to miraculous signs include: Pisidian Antioch (Acts 13); the women in Philippi (Acts 16); Thessalonica, Berea and Athens (Acts 17); Corinth (Acts 18); Jerusalem, including Paul's preaching to the mob (Acts 22), and the Sanhedrin (Acts 23); Caesarea, including Paul's hearings before Felix (Acts 24), Festus (Acts 25) and Agrippa (Acts 26).

Similarly, in letters such as those written to Timothy, in which Paul encourages and prepares him for the work of preaching and leading in the church, no mention is made of miraculous signs. It seems that in the early days of the church, God gave miraculous signs along with the preaching of the gospel to prove that the apostles, like Jesus Christ, were truly sent from God. But as the authority of the apostles became established, the need for accompanying miracles diminished. In fact, they began to cause problems, when people became more interested in the signs than the message, as Paul's experience in Corinth shows.

4. Who is unable to understand the message (v 6, 8, 14)? Why? The rulers of this age (v 6 and 8); the man without the Spirit (v 14). They cannot understand or accept this message because…

a. it does not follow the wisdom of this age (v 6) and so appears foolish to them (v 14).

b. it is beyond the powers of human reason or imagination (v 9) to understand this message.

5. Who can understand the message (v 14-15)? Why? Those to whom God has revealed it by His Spirit, because it can only be spiritually discerned (v 14). Notice that these people are not cleverer or better than those who do not understand God's message. They are simply those who have been freely given the Spirit by God (v 12), implying that they have done nothing to earn or deserve this. Similarly, the "person with the Spirit" (v 15) is not describing a person who is naturally more attuned to God and the supernatural, but simply one who has been given the Spirit by God.

6. Why do we need the Spirit to understand God's message (v 10-11)? The Spirit is the only one who knows the thoughts of God (v 10-11). Notice how the reference to all three persons of the Trinity is completed in v 16—those who understand God's message by the Spirit have "the mind of Christ".

7. In what form does God's message come to us, according to verse 13? Verse 13 shows us that God's message is communicated in words—"words taught by the Spirit". This is important because many believe that God's message comes to us in two ways—the words of the Bible and then, additionally, through dreams, pictures,

impressions and experiences given by the Spirit.

EXPLORE MORE:
Read the following Bible passages. How do they agree with what we have learned so far?

• **2 Peter 1 v 20-21:** Prophecies of Scripture didn't come from the minds of men, but from God (compare 1 Corinthians 2 v 9-10). Men spoke (ie: words) from God and it was the Holy Spirit that enabled them to do this (compare 1 Corinthians 2 v 13). Some people imagine that God spoke to the prophets, who then spoke to the people and passed on God's message. But that is not the process of revelation described here. Rather, God spoke to the people through the words that the prophets were speaking.

• **Hebrews 1 v 1-2:** God has spoken (ie: words), both through the prophets of old and now, supremely, by His Son (compare 1 Corinthians 2 v 1-2).

• **1 Peter 1 v 10-12:** God didn't speak different messages through the prophets and then through His Son. When the prophets spoke the words of God by the Holy Spirit, they were speaking about Jesus Christ, His sufferings and "the glories that would follow" (compare 1 Corinthians 2 v 2).

8. APPLY: Is it possible to know God? How? It is possible, but only because He has revealed Himself to us. We can only know God through the message about Jesus Christ. He is God's supreme and final revelation ("in these last days"—Hebrews 1 v 2). But, in order to accept the message about Jesus Christ, we need to receive God's Spirit—without the Spirit this message will just seem foolish and we won't be able to understand it (1 Corinthians 2 v 14).

9. APPLY: How should this affect:

• our response to the message about Jesus Christ? (See also John 14 v 23-24 and Hebrews 2 v 1.) We need to ask God to give us His Spirit, so that we can accept and understand His words about Jesus Christ. John 14 v 23-24: We must obey the teaching of Jesus, which comes from God the Father. Hebrews 2 v 1: We must pay careful attention to what we have heard.

• our attitude to academics and so-called experts who look down on Christian beliefs? Christians should not be intimidated by those who reject God's message, however impressive their academic credentials may appear. They may have "human wisdom" but that is utterly useless in discerning what God has said. Like all of us, they need God's Spirit to accept the message about Jesus Christ.

• the way we share God's message with others? We need to pray that God will give His Spirit to those who hear it, so that they can understand and accept it. We can't share about Jesus without the help of God. Nor should we be tempted to teach about anything other than Jesus.

However outdated or counter-cultural the message seems, it alone is the revelation of God to our world—nothing else will do.

10. What was the role of the Spirit in the production of the Old Testament? Look at the following Bible passages and complete the table. See table below. If people do not have access to footnotes in a Bible, you will need to help with answers in column three.

11. How has God spoken to us in these last days (Hebrews 1 v 2), and what is the role of the Spirit in that? Look at the following Bible passages and complete the table. See table on next page.

12. So what should our attitude be to the Old Testament? Both Jesus and the apostles taught that the words of the OT prophets were spoken by the Holy Spirit Himself. 1 Peter 1 v 10-12 shows us that the Old Testament is a "Spirit production" for the benefit of Christians. In the Old Testament the Spirit reveals the same things as in the New Testament. It is a revelation about Jesus Christ—"he [the Holy Spirit] predicted the sufferings of the Messiah and

	Who's speaking/ writing?	Who is being quoted?	What is said about the Spirit?
Matthew 22 v 43	Jesus	David (Psalm 110)	David spoke this by the Spirit
Acts 1 v 16	Peter	David (Psalms 69 and 109)	The Spirit spoke through the mouth of David
Acts 28 v 25	Paul	Isaiah (ch. 6)	The Spirit spoke through Isaiah
Hebrews 3 v 7	Unknown	Writer of Psalm 95	The Spirit says this
Hebrews 10 v 15	Unknown	Jeremiah	The Spirit says this

	Who does the Spirit help?	What does the Spirit do?
John 3 v 31-34	Jesus	Jesus speaks the words of God because God has given Him the Spirit "without limit" (v 34).
John 14 v 16-26	The disciples (minus Judas, who had already left), who would be given the task of taking Jesus' teaching to the whole world (Acts 1 v 8).	• He will live in them (v 17). • He will teach them "all things" and remind them of everything Jesus has said to them (v 26).

the glories that would follow" (v 11); "they [the Old Testament prophets] spoke of the things that have now been told you by those who have preached the gospel to you by the Holy Spirit" (v 12).

Note: There are, however, important differences between the Old and New Testaments. God's revelation in Scripture is progressive (ie: we don't find out everything that He wants us to know in the OT alone). We need the NT.

And what should our attitude be to the New Testament? Both the words of Jesus and the teaching of His apostles come by the Spirit. We can be confident that there is no difference in content, accuracy or trustworthiness. Because of the Spirit, the disciples would be supernaturally reminded of everything that Jesus had taught, and Jesus' words were not His own but the words of God the Father.

13. How does [2 Tim 3 v 16-17] agree with what we have learned so far about how God reveals Himself? It completes the final part of the picture by showing us that not only the spoken words of Jesus and the apostles, but also the Scriptures— the written words of the Old Testament prophets and the New Testament apostles that we now have in the Bible—are the words of God Himself. Many Christians believe that while the Bible has an important place in revealing God's message to us, it

is also desirable that the church receives contemporary messages through prophecies, visions etc. given by the Spirit. However, since the Scriptures thoroughly equip us for every good work, it is clear that God has already told us everything we need to know.

• **Look at v 16. What do you think "God-breathed" means?** Try to say a word without using a breath, either in or out— it's not possible. "God-breathed" means the same as "by the Spirit". God's breath and God's Spirit are linked in the Bible. See Job 33 v 4 and 34 v 14-15; John 20 v 22.

• **Look at v 17. What can the Scripture do for us? So do we need more revelation from God?** "The man of God may be thoroughly equipped for every good work." This suggests that no more is needed.

14. APPLY: Summarise what you have learned about the Spirit and the Bible. Give people an opportunity to share what they have learned in this first session.

• **How do people carve up the Bible into parts that are trustworthy or relevant, and parts that are not? Why is that wrong?** Many people, including Christians, regard the Old Testament as the inferior part of the Bible. They believe that it has been completely superseded by the New Testament, and is now totally irrelevant for Christians. But this was certainly not the view of Jesus or the apostles (see Q10 above). Other people draw a distinction between the words of Jesus and of the apostles, particularly Paul. This has given rise to ideas such as the theory that Paul had a different agenda to Jesus and effectively hi-jacked Christianity after the time of Jesus. Similarly, red-letter Bibles, where the words of Jesus are printed in red ink, seem to suggest that Jesus' teaching is more reliable and important than that of the apostles. But the New Testament is clear that the Spirit, by whom Jesus spoke the words of God, is the same Spirit who reminded Jesus' followers of everything He had taught them (see Q11 above), and the same Spirit who had helped the Old Testament prophets to predict Christ. Since all parts of the Bible—Old Testament, Jesus' teaching and apostles' teaching—have been communicated by the Spirit, all parts of the Bible are equally the words of God.

• **How do Christians sometimes separate the Spirit from God's word, the Bible? Why is that wrong?** Some Christians today accept the Bible as the foundation of Christian belief, but also believe that God continues to give new revelations through the Spirit that are separate from the Scriptures and come by other means, such as dreams, pictures, impressions, "co-incidences" and experiences. (People often claim that these revelations are subject to the Bible, but because they are more spectacular they tend to become more significant.) 1 Corinthians 2 however, shows that God's message to our world is "in words taught by the Spirit" (v 13) and we have seen how each part of the Scriptures has come into being as the Spirit speaks God's words through humans. In the Bible, God's Spirit and God's word go together. And 2 Timothy 3 v 17 shows us that we need nothing else.

2 Various
THE SPIRIT AND THE OT

THE BIG IDEA
In the OT the Spirit wasn't given to all God's people, but the OT promised both a single "Spirit Person", and many "Spirit people", who would all have the Spirit; this was fulfilled in the NT, in Jesus and His church.

SUMMARY
The purpose of this session is to compare Old and New Testament teaching about the Spirit. To do this it is necessary to understand the purpose of the Old Testament. If, as many people do, we treat passages from the Old and New Testaments in the same way, and apply Old Testament references directly to ourselves, we will fall into error. Instead, we need to understand that the Old Testament was given to prepare the way for God's salvation and Saviour.

The Old Testament shows humanity's utter need for God's salvation. Over hundreds of years it shows us that every other way of dealing with human sin and trying to bring people into a relationship with

God—catastrophic judgments like the flood, miraculous experiences like the exodus, the law, the tabernacle, judges, kings etc—has failed. (Note: God planned for these things to fail so that we could understand our urgent need that only Jesus Christ can meet.) As the "failures" accumulate, a picture builds up of what humans truly need if they are to be God's people. At the same time, promises of what God will do in the future both multiply and increase in splendour, even as the political nation of Israel declines. God has planned something greater and better, and the New Testament reveals that to be Jesus Christ.

From this, it follows that:

a. We should not expect the gift of the Spirit in the Old Testament to be the same as the gift of the Spirit to Christians, because the Old Testament is the time of "unfulfilment", whereas we live in the time of fulfilment of God's promises.

b. We should not be able to speak of the Holy Spirit, without speaking of Christ, to whom the whole Old Testament points and in whom all the Old Testament promises are fulfilled.

The Bible passages investigated in this session aim to make the following points:

- In the Old Testament only specially chosen individuals were given the Spirit, in order to carry out specific tasks—constructing/planning the tabernacle/temple, leading God's people and prophesying God's word.
- In the Old Testament individuals who were given the Spirit could also have the Spirit withdrawn by God.
- The Old Testament recognises, in the heartfelt wish of Moses and the promises of Ezekiel, that a better and greater gift of the Spirit to God's people was to come.
- The Old Testament prophet Isaiah promises

a special "Spirit Person"—He would be God's anointed Servant King, who would bring both God's justice and good news for God's people.

- The Old Testament prophets Ezekiel and Joel promise a new Spirit people, to whom the Spirit would be given; He would cleanse them, give them a new heart and spirit, enable them to follow God's laws, bring them to life again, live in them, bring them into God's promised land, and enable all of them to prophesy.
- The New Testament books of Luke and Acts show that Jesus Christ fulfils the promises of a special Spirit Person, and that He Himself is the Spirit-Giver, pouring out the Spirit on His apostles and all those who repent and turn to Him.
- The New Testament shows that Christians fulfil the promises of the new Spirit people—all kinds of people are baptised by the Spirit into one body (the church), are cleansed and given new birth by the Spirit, and are controlled by the Spirit, who lives in them.
- Those who do not have the Spirit do not belong to Christ, and no one can be a Christian except by the Holy Spirit.

GUIDANCE FOR QUESTIONS

1. It has been said that we must interpret the Old Testament in the light of the New Testament. Give some examples of what happens if we don't follow this advice. If people struggle with answering this question, give some examples of the wrong thinking that can result; for example:

- All Christian males should be circumcised!
- We should stone adulterers.

The point of this question is to expose the error of applying to ourselves today what God said to Israel in the Old Testament, without first looking at the New Testament as well. In the same way, we need to understand the working of the Spirit in the Old Testament through the fuller revelation of the New Testament.

2. Look up the following verses and answer the questions given in the table. See table below. You may like to divide up this question (and others like it) for different pairs or sub-groups to answer and then report back.

3. What three types of activity were carried out by those who were given the Spirit in the Old Testament?

- constructing/planning the tabernacle/ temple
- leading God's people

- prophesying God's word. (Prophecy in the Old Testament is not just about prediction, although some prophets predicted events; it's about speaking God's word—usually the law—to the people of the day eg: Moses was a great prophet, but he was known for bringing God's law to His people, not for his predictions.)

Note: You may need to beware of people jumping to the conclusion that the Spirit is given as inspiration for our artistic endeavours. As we have already seen, these Old Testament references cannot be applied directly to ourselves.

Note: Questions 4-5 below highlight aspects of the work of the Spirit in the Old Testament, that, later in this session, will be

	Who had the Spirit?	What did they do?
a. Exodus 31 v 1-7	Bezalel (a craftsman)	Made the tabernacle and its furnishings
b. Num 11 v 16-17	70 elders	Helped Moses to lead Israel
c. Deut 34 v 9 (see NIV footnote)	Joshua	Became leader of Israel, like Moses
d. Judges 3 v 7-11	Othniel	Became a judge and led Israel to victory against the enemies
e. Judges 15 v 11-15	Samson	Defeated the enemies of Israel
f. 1 Sam 10 v 1, 6, 9-11	Saul	Prophesied
g. 1 Sam 16 v 13	David	Became king
h. 2 Sam 23 v 1-2	David	Prophesied
i. 1 Chron 28 v 11-12	David	Planned the temple
j. 2 Chron 24 v 20	Zechariah, son of Jehoiada	Prophesied
k. Ezek 2 v 1-8	Ezekiel	Prophesied
l. Zech 7 v 12	The earlier prophets	Prophesied
m. Luke 1 v 67	Zechariah, father of John	Prophesied

found to be different from the work of the Spirit in the New Testament.

4. Look at Moses' response to Joshua. How does this answer the question of who received God's Spirit in the OT? What does Moses' heartfelt wish tell us? Numbers 11 v 29 shows us that the Spirit was not given to all the Lord's people. In this case, He was only given to those chosen to help Moses in the task of leading God's people ie: very few of the Lord's people. But Moses' desire was that all of God's people could have the Spirit, indicating something greater and better than Israel's experience of the Holy Spirit up to that time. What that greater and better experience could be will become clearer as we investigate the promises about the Spirit given in the Old Testament (see Q7 onwards).

5. What does this verse tell us about the gift of the Spirit in the Old Testament (see also Psalm 51 v 11)? The Spirit was given to Saul when he was anointed by Samuel as the first king of Israel (1 Samuel 10 v 1 and 6), but because of Saul's repeated disobedience to God's word the Spirit finally left him. As Saul's experience shows, just because a person had once received the Spirit, it didn't necessarily mean that they would always have the Spirit.

6. Look up the following verses and answer the questions given in the table. See table below.

7. Look up the following verses and answer the questions given in the table. See table at top of next page.

8. Look at the following verses and answer the questions given in the table. See second table on next page.

	How is the Spirit-filled person described?	What will the Spirit-filled person do?
Isaiah 11 v 1-5	A king—"from the stump of Jesse" (v 1) means from the family of King David (see 2 Samuel 7 v 12 –13).	• Delight in the fear of the Lord (v 3) • Judge with justice (v 3-4) • Uphold the poor (v 4) • Slay the wicked (v 4)
Isaiah 42 v 1-4	God's servant (v 1)	• Bring justice to the nations (v 1); not falter until justice is established (v 4) • Not shout or cry out (v 2) • Not be destructive (v 3) • Give his law (v 4)
Isaiah 61 v 1-3	Anointed by God (v 1)	• Bring good news to the poor (v 1) • Help the brokenhearted (v 1) • Release prisoners (v 1) • Proclaim the Lord's favour (v 2) • Proclaim God's vengeance (v 2) • Bring joy to God's people who mourn (v 3)

	Who is the Spirit given to?	What will the Spirit do?
Ezekiel 36 v 24-27	Israel (see v 22) ie: God's people	• Cleanse them from all their impurities (v 25) • Give them a new heart and spirit (v 26) • Help them to follow God's laws (v 27)
Ezekiel 37 v 1-14	The whole house of Israel (v 11) ie: God's people	• Bring them to life again (v 13) • Live in them (v 14) • Settle them in their own land (v 14)
Ezekiel 39 v 25-29	Jacob (v 25), Israel (v 29) ie: God's people	• Bring them back from captivity (v 25) • Show God's face among them (v 29)
Joel 2 v 28-32	All people (v 28)	The Spirit will: • enable all kinds of people to prophesy (v 28)

	Who is the promised Spirit person?	What does He do?
Luke 3 v 16-17	Jesus	He will baptise with the Holy Spirit (v 16)
Luke 3 v 21-22	Jesus, God's Son	He is pleasing to God
Luke 4 v 16-21	Jesus	He fulfils the prophecy of Isaiah 61 v 1-2
Acts 1 v 4-5	Jesus	He baptises His apostles with the Holy Spirit
Acts 2 v 32-33	Jesus	He has received the Spirit from the Father and poured Him out on His apostles.
Acts 2 v 38-39	Jesus	He provides forgiveness and the Spirit to all those who repent and are baptised in His name

9. Who are the promised Spirit people and how are the OT promises about them fulfilled? (Use the table in Q7 above to remind yourself of the OT promises.) *1 Cor 12 v 13:* Compare Joel 2 v 28-29 and 32. The promised Spirit people are the church. All kinds of people—whether Jews or Greeks, slave or free—are baptised by the Spirit into one body, so God's people are no longer confined to the nation of Israel, and those who have the Spirit are no longer confined to specially chosen individuals such as prophets, judges or kings.

Note: Baptism with the Spirit is covered in Session Three.

Romans 8 v 9: Christians are in the realm of (or controlled by, NIV84) the Spirit (compare Ezekiel 36 v 27) and God's Spirit lives in them (compare Ezekiel 37 v 14). Note that all those who do not have the Spirit do not belong to Christ. In other words, to be a Christian you must have the Spirit.

Titus 3 v 4-7: Those who are saved by God receive the Spirit, who cleanses them (compare Ezekiel 36 v 25) and gives them new birth (compare Ezekiel 37 v 13). Note that it is through Jesus Christ that the Spirit is poured out.

10. How does the Spirit come to the promised Spirit people? The Spirit comes to Christians through Jesus Christ. The promised Spirit Person is also the Spirit-Giver. See Jesus' words to His apostles in John 14 v 26 and 16 v 7. The Spirit is the gift of the Father to His Son, that Jesus then gives to His people. We can say that the gift of the Spirit is both from the Father and from Jesus.

11. How does Jesus use the themes from Ezekiel (see Q7 above) to show that being a Christian is much more than a matter of intellectual religious belief (v 3-8)? Jesus tells Nicodemus that no one can see or enter the kingdom of God unless he is born again, of water and the Spirit. In saying this, He echoes the words of Ezek 36 v 25-27, where God promises to sprinkle clean water on His people and cleanse them from all their impurities (v 25), and to put His Spirit in them (v 27), thus giving them a new heart and a new spirit (v 26) that will move them to keep His laws (v 27). The problem in Ezekiel's time was that God's people had hearts of stone (v 26) that could not be moved to keep His laws, and it was no different in the time of Nicodemus. Although Nicodemus was a Pharisee, Jesus was telling him that even his law-keeping wasn't enough. He too needed the work of the Spirit, as promised in Ezekiel.

12. Look at the following verses (v 9-16). How does Jesus relate this work of the Spirit to His own work? Jesus goes on to tell Nicodemus that:
• He has come from heaven and speaks of what He knows and has seen (v 11-13).

• He must be "lifted up" (crucified), just as Moses lifted up the bronze snake in the desert, to save those being punished by God (see Numbers 21 v 8-9).
• everyone who believes in Him will not perish but have eternal life.
To have eternal life in God's kingdom, we must believe in Jesus Christ and be born again by the Spirit.

13. APPLY: How would you respond to someone who seeks to live by the teachings of Jesus, and has deep respect for Him as a great teacher and prophet, but knows nothing about the Holy Spirit? Nicodemus seems to have respect for Jesus as a great teacher and prophet, but the words of Jesus in John 3 v 3-8 show clearly that Nicodemus was not able to enter the kingdom of God. This requires more than simply an attitude of respect for Jesus and an interest in Him—it requires a divine work of God that Jesus calls being "born again" (v 3) or being "born of water and the Spirit" (v 5). A person who seeks to follow Jesus, however sincerely, without knowing anything of the Spirit, or just ignoring the Spirit, clearly has no idea of what Jesus came to do or of what it means to be a true Christian. We need to help this person understand the gospel.

• **Comment on this statment: "I see the Spirit as a divine inspiration that allows me to express myself creatively in art and music, through which I can glorify God."** This idea may well come from accounts of Old Testament craftsmen such as Bezalel (see Q2), who were given the Spirit to enable them to complete the tabernacle to the supremely high standards set by God. However, these are not passages for us to apply directly to ourselves. That would ignore the fact that the Old Testament promises and yearns for a time of greater and better things that are fulfilled in the New Testament. The greater and better thing is Jesus Christ—the promised Spirit Person, who pours out the Spirit on all His followers—the promised Spirit people. The great work of the Spirit in the Bible is not about artistic inspiration but the new life that we receive when we repent and turn to Jesus Christ, without which we can do nothing to glorify God.

- **Comment on this statement: "I went to a three-hour Holy Spirit meeting where many strange things happened, but Jesus wasn't mentioned."** The New Testament shows that Jesus fulfils the Old Testament promises of both a "Spirit Person" (He is baptised with the Holy Spirit) and of a new "Spirit people" (He baptises His apostles with the Spirit and gives the Spirit to all those who repent and turn to Him for forgiveness of sins). The fact that Jesus isn't mentioned at all in a "Holy Spirit meeting" should raise serious doubts about whether the meeting has anything to do with the Spirit at all.

3 Acts 2 v 1–41
BAPTISED WITH THE SPIRIT

THE BIG IDEA
The first baptism of the Spirit took place on the day of Pentecost, which in one sense was a unique foundational event in the history of the church; subsequently baptism with the Spirit = becoming a Christian.

SUMMARY
The aim of this session is to show that:
- Jesus is the Spirit King, enthroned in heaven, and He is the one who pours out His Spirit on His people.
- baptism of the Spirit happens when someone repents and believes in Jesus.

There are a number of errors that commonly occur in the thinking of people on this subject.
- Some people believe that baptism with the Spirit is something separate to becoming a Christian. Such people would say that you may be saved, but are still in need of a "second blessing" of baptism with the Spirit, which will make you a "Spirit-filled Christian". But it will be seen that the New Testament is clear—you cannot be saved without receiving baptism with the Spirit.
- Books, conferences, sermons, conversations and even ministries on the Spirit abound. Many Christians will come across, at some time or other, people or churches who constantly speak about the Spirit, Spirit-filled people and Spirit-filled ministry. It should ring alarm bells if all we hear is about the Spirit and not about Jesus Christ. In the New Testament, the great sign of the Spirit's work is that Jesus is centre-stage, not the Spirit.
- Some people focus on the supernatural wonders that accompanied the first baptism with the Spirit on the day of Pentecost—tongues of fire, the sound of a mighty wind and the ability to speak in different tongues. Such people often seek these phenomena for themselves, and look for them in the life of every believer, particularly speaking in tongues. The

point of these supernatural happenings, as always in the Bible, is that they were signs, pointing away from themselves to something far greater that was happening at the time. On the day of Pentecost the supernatural phenomena were fireworks of the enthronement of Jesus Christ—signs that Jesus had been exalted to the highest position in the universe. We shouldn't be seeking the signs but the greater reality to which they point.

The Bible passages investigated in this session set out the following points:

• The baptism with the Spirit, promised by Jesus, first took place on the day of Pentecost, as recorded in Acts 2.

• These events fulfilled the prophecy of Joel 2 v 28-32.

• The outpouring of the Spirit on the day of Pentecost was a sign of Jesus' enthronement in heaven as Lord and Christ (Acts 2 v 33-36).

• Baptism with the Spirit leads to proclamation of the truth about Jesus Christ; this is the "prophesying" mentioned in Joel 2.

• Baptism with the Spirit leads some of those who hear the proclamation of the gospel to seek help, repent, receive for themselves the gift of the Spirit and join the church (Acts 2 v 37-41).

• The New Testament subsequently teaches that all Christians are baptised by the Spirit (1 Corinthians 12 v 13).

GUIDANCE FOR QUESTIONS

1. Give examples of words or phrases that have completely different meanings when used by different generations or social groups. Examples include: wicked (bad, really good); gay (light-hearted, homosexual, embarrassingly pathetic); surf (ride waves, use the internet) etc.

Note: The term "baptism with the Spirit" is not used in Acts 2, but Qs 2 and 3 aim to show clearly that this is the correct term to describe the events of the day of Pentecost.

2. What do these two verses tell us about when the baptism with the Holy Spirit promised by Jesus took place?
• **Acts 1 v 5:** looks forward to the baptism with the Spirit—"in a few days".

• **Acts 11 v 15-17:** Peter is explaining to the other apostles how the first non-Jews had come to faith in Christ, and looks back to the baptism with the Spirit that the apostles had received—"God gave them the same gift as he gave us". So the first baptism with the Spirit occurred between these two Bible references.

3. Scan the chapters of Acts, between 1 v 5 and 11 v 15-17 to find out precisely when this event took place. This question will be most helpful to those who are not very familiar with Acts. Give people just a few minutes to do this; if they look at the section headings in a version such as NIV, they will quickly see that the first baptism with the Spirit is in Acts 2. Pentecost occurred a few days after Jesus had spoken to His apostles, and similar events later took place after Peter had preached the Christian message to the household of Cornelius (see Acts 10). This is what he is speaking about to the other apostles in Acts 11.

4. List everything that happened [in 2 v 1-13, 41]. The main events were:
• a sound like a violent wind (v 2)
• tongues of fire (v 3)
• Jesus' followers speaking in other tongues as the Spirit enabled them (v 4) and declaring the wonders of God in many languages (v 11)

- people who heard them were amazed (v 7, 12)
- some people made fun of them (v 13)
- people who accepted Peter's message (about 3,000 of them) were baptised and joined the church.

5. What did people at the time understand to be the meaning of the events that they had witnessed (see v 12-13)? When people were witnessing these events, before Peter stood up and explained them, some were perplexed and asked "What does this mean?" (v 12). Others decided that the apostles must be drunk (v 13). Note that no one correctly understood what was happening until Peter had explained the meaning. It may be worth asking your group: If Peter hadn't explained these events, how might you have interpreted them?

6. How do the events of the day of Pentecost fulfil the promises, found in Joel 2 v 28-32, that Peter quotes [in Acts 2 v 14-21]? The believers prophesied because of the Spirit—compare Joel 2 v 28 and Acts 2 v 4; people called on the name of the Lord and were saved—compare Joel 2 v 32 and Acts 2 v 38-41.

Regarding the prophecy of wonders in heaven above and signs on the earth below, we need to remember that Joel was speaking in what is called an "apocalyptic" style—a very vivid language about last days and grand events. The sun was not literally darkened nor the moon turned to blood; in the same way, Joel's prophecy didn't mean that everyone dreamed a dream on the day of Pentecost. Joel wrote in picture language about the fact that from Pentecost onwards ("in the last days"—Acts 2 v 17), all kinds of people, whether young or old, male or female, rich or poor, would be able to speak

the truth about Jesus (see Hebrews 1 v 1-2). It was a fulfilment of the desire of Moses (Numbers 11 v 29) that not just prophets and leaders, but every one of God's people would have the Spirit.

7. Imagine that you were in the crowd that witnessed these events. What might you expect people to talk about? (See Acts 2 v 7-8.) v 7-8 suggests that what struck people most was the fact that uneducated Jewish men from Galilee were able to speak fluently and comprehensibly in so many different languages. The impression we get is that they were more interested in finding out how this had happened than in listening to what was actually being said. Similarly today, it's often the speaking in tongues that captures people's attention when they read or hear or talk about the baptism with the Spirit on the day of Pentecost.

8. What does Peter talk about? Jesus. **List the main points in his sermon.**
- Jesus was accredited by God through miracles (v 22)
- Jesus was handed over to the Jews in accordance with God's plan (v 23)
- the Jews were responsible for Jesus' death (v 23)
- God raised Jesus from death (v 24)
- Jesus' resurrection was predicted in the Old Testament (v 25-31)
- the apostles are witnesses of Jesus' resurrection (v 32)
- Jesus is exalted at God's right hand (v 33)
- Jesus has poured out the Spirit (v 33)
- Jesus' exaltation was predicted in the Old Testament (v 34-35)
- God has made Jesus Lord and Christ (v 36).

Notice that it's all about Jesus, not the Holy Spirit.

9. What event, according to Peter, shows that Jesus is now alive and exalted in heaven, even though the audience cannot see Him? Jesus receives the Spirit from the Father and pours Him out on His followers (v 33). This happened when Jesus was exalted to the right hand of God. The visible and audible wonders that accompanied the Spirit's arrival were signs that the enthronement of Jesus had taken place; just as, in the time of the exodus, the pillar of cloud and pillar of fire signified visibly that God was with His people. At Jesus' baptism, the dove showed that God's Spirit had come down upon him. In Acts 4, the shaking of the building showed that God had heard the believers' prayer and the Spirit had come to help them. At times, the Spirit gives demonstrations of His presence and power that can be seen, heard or felt. At other times nothing like that happens.

10. Why were the people cut to the heart? They understood that they were responsible for crucifying the one that God had made Lord and Christ.

11. Why was Peter's message good news? If they repented and were baptised in the name of Jesus, they would receive forgiveness and the gift of the Holy Spirit.

12. What is promised in verses 38-39? Who is this for? Forgiveness of sins and the gift of the Spirit is for everyone who repents—whether these people, their families, or "all who are far off" (v 39).

13. What do the events of the day of Pentecost show us about the work of the Spirit... • in regard to Jesus? The Holy Spirit shows the glory of Christ, demonstrating that He has been exalted to God's right hand and made Lord and Christ.

• in regard to the apostles? The Holy Spirit helps them to proclaim the truth about Jesus. Peter, an uneducated fisherman, was able to teach about Jesus, and confidently use OT Scriptures; notice too his boldness (v 36), compared with his cowardice at the trial of Jesus. The baptism of the Spirit had transformed him.

• in regard to the audience? The Spirit helped many to become Christians. 3,000 people, who originally were perplexed and even mocking (v 12-13), responded to Peter's message by repenting and being baptised in the name of Jesus Christ.

14. After the day of Pentecost, who is baptised with the Spirit? And what is the effect of baptism with the Spirit (see also v 3)? All Christians are baptised with the Spirit. The effect is to unite many different kinds of people into one body, the church (v 13), under the lordship of Jesus Christ (v 3). So baptism with the Spirit = becoming a Christian ie: repenting and believing in Jesus Christ for the forgiveness of sins.

15. APPLY: What would you expect to see in someone who claims to have been baptised with the Spirit? You should expect to find that they have repented of their old way of life and turned to Jesus Christ for the forgiveness of their sins, that they give Jesus Christ lordship and centre-stage in their life, and that they are united with other Christians.

• "No one can say, 'Jesus is Lord,' except by the Holy Spirit" (1 Cor 12 v 3). Why not? Because only the Spirit knows the thoughts of God, the truth about Jesus, which cannot be grasped by human wisdom/imagination, can only be revealed to us by the Spirit (1 Cor 2 v 7-14).

4 Acts (various)
THE GIFT OF THE SPIRIT

THE BIG IDEA
The gift of the Spirit = baptism with the Spirit = becoming a Christian.

SUMMARY
The aim of this session is to demonstrate conclusively that all the references to the gift / baptism / receiving / pouring out etc. of the Spirit in Acts are referring to the same thing—He is given when the good news about Jesus Christ is preached, heard and responded to in repentance and faith. This view is supported both by the teaching of Paul in Titus 3 v 4-7 and the words of Jesus in John 3 v 1-16.

Many Christians believe that the gift of the Spirit is something separate from salvation; it is a special empowering of the Spirit, usually to help people carry out a particular ministry that will have great effect. As we saw in Session Two, this is what happened when the Spirit was given in the Old Testament. However, a survey of the New Testament shows that this is a wrong understanding of the gift of the Spirit to Christians.

Note: The gift of the Spirit mustn't be confused with the gifts of the Spirit, which we will look at in Session Seven.

This session will show that:
- there are a number of different terms that refer to the gift of the Spirit in Acts—baptised, came on, filled with, poured out, received etc.
- the gift of the Spirit is for those who repent and believe in Jesus.
- the gift of the Spirit in Acts comes as a result of preaching or explaining the Christian message.

- in Acts, the gift of the Spirit is sometimes accompanied by phenomena like speaking in tongues or healing, but not always.
- Titus 3 v 4-7 explains further the same gift of the Spirit that is described in Acts, and shows that this gift is for all who repent and believe in Jesus.
- the gift of the Spirit is the same as being born again (John 3 v 3-6).

GUIDANCE FOR QUESTIONS
1. What do most people think when they hear the term "born again Christian"? What about you? Allow people to share from their own experience. In our culture, the term "born-again Christian" has become synonymous with "weirdo" or "fanatical fundamentalist". Hopefully, this session will help people to appreciate the astonishing wonder of what it means to be truly born again.

2. Look up the following verses and answer the questions given in the table. See the table on the next page. To save time, you can divide your group into pairs or sub-groups and allocate one or more references to each.

Acts...	What words describe the giving of the Spirit?	Who is the Spirit given to?	What led to this?	Are there any other events connected with this?
1 v 4-5	baptised (note also "gift" v 4)	Jesus' followers	God's promise	
1 v 8	comes on you			Jesus says they will be His witnesses to the ends of the earth.
2 v 4	filled with			Wind, tongues of fire and ability to speak in different languages.
2 v 33	poured out	Given to Jesus to give to His followers.	Jesus' exaltation at the right hand of God	The crowd could now see and hear that Jesus had been made Lord and Christ (v 33-36).
2 v 38	receive the gift	Anyone who repents and is baptised in the name of Jesus Christ for the forgiveness of sins.enemies of Israel	Listeners were cut to the heart and asked Peter what they should do (v 37).	About 3,000 people accepted the message, were baptised and joined the church (v 41).
8 v 15	receive	Samaritan believers	(v 12) They believed Philip as he preached the good news and were baptised.	(v 15, 17) Peter and John prayed for them and placed hands on them.
8 v 16	come upon			
8 v 17	received			
9 v 17	filled with	Saul/Paul	(v 4-6, 17) Jesus appeared to Saul; Ananias explained to Saul what had happened and	Scales fell from Saul's eyes and he could see again (v 18); then he was baptised.
10 v 44	came on	Cornelius and household— the first Gentile believers	Peter's preaching	They spoke in tongues and praised God.
10 v 45	poured out			
10 v 47	received			

11 v 15	came on			(v 18) God had granted Gentiles repentance that leads to life.
11 v 16	baptised with			
11 v 17	gift			
15 v 8	giving			v 9 God purified their hearts by faith.
19 v 6	came on	(v 1-5) The disciples who had only received John's baptism.	(v 2) The apostles asked them about the Spirit.	They were baptised in the name of Jesus. After receiving the Spirit, they spoke in tongues and prophesied

3. What do you notice about the words used for the giving of the Spirit? There are a number of terms—gift, baptised with, came on, filled with, poured out, and received—that refer to the giving of the Spirit, and are used interchangeably throughout the book of Acts.

4. In each incident... • what happens before the gift of the Spirit (apart from the first three references in the table)? Christians are preaching, explaining or witnessing to the good news about Christ.

• **what is always the response from others?** Among those who hear the good news, there are always people who repent, accept the message, and are baptised (ie: become Christians).

Because these things are always mentioned wherever Acts describes the giving of the Spirit, we should also expect them to be part of any baptism / filling / pouring out of the Spirit that happens now.

5. Which features only occur sometimes? Wind and tongues of fire (Acts 2 v 2-3); speaking in tongues leading to praising God / prophesying (Acts 2 v 4, 10 v 46, Acts 19 v 6); laying on of hands (Acts 8 v 17); physical healing (Acts 9 v 18). **What does this tell us?** Not to automatically equate these things with the gift of the Spirit; sometimes they may occur, and sometimes not. The Spirit may be given without any of these special signs taking place.

6. APPLY: If someone says to you that you can't have received the Spirit because you don't speak in tongues, or because no one has laid hands on you, how would you respond? You need to show them that in Acts there was no set formula for the giving of the Spirit. Eg: there were also several occasions when people received the gift of the Spirit and didn't speak in tongues eg: Acts 2 v 38-41, Acts 8 v 17, Acts 9 v 17-18. On the other hand, you need to show them the words of Peter in Acts 2 v 38-39; the qualification for receiving the gift of the Spirit is repentance and turning to Jesus Christ for forgiveness. The question you need to ask yourself is: have I done this? If the answer is yes, then according to Peter, you can be confident that you have received the gift of the Spirit.

7. From the verses that we have looked at in Acts, is it correct to say that receiving the gift of the Spirit = becoming a Christian? Yes. However, at this stage some people will still be unconvinced, probably because this understanding of "gift of the Spirit" may be very different from what they were previously taught and have been wrongly reading into Scripture until now. The truth that the gift of the Spirit = becoming a Christian will be confirmed in the next part of the session, by looking at other parts of the New Testament that explain (rather than simply describe) the gift of the Spirit.

8. What is being explained in these verses [Titus 3 v 4-7]? What happens when someone repents and believes in Jesus (v 5—"he (God) saved us").

9. What is similar to the passages from Acts? v 5-6—"the Holy Spirit, whom he poured out on us generously through Jesus Christ our Saviour".

10. What else do we learn about what the Holy Spirit does for us? Write down all the benefits of receiving the gift of the Spirit—and take time to appreciate how wonderful God's gift to us is. Paul tells us that by the Holy Spirit, those of us who are saved…
- receive the washing of rebirth and renewal (v 5).
- have been justified by God's grace (v 7).
- can become heirs having the hope of eternal life (v 7).
To help your group to really understand and revel in what is being said here, you might like to ask some optional extra questions. Or if time is short, you can summarise these points. But it's important to help people rejoice in them.

⊻

- **What were we like before God saved us?** See verse 3.

- **Why did God save us?** (See verse 5.)
- **What does it mean to be washed, reborn and renewed (v 5)?**
- **What does it mean to be justified by God's grace (v 7)?** You may need to explain "justified" (declared not guilty) and "grace" (God's kindness and mercy to those who don't deserve it).
- **How has the future changed for those who are saved?** See verse 7.
- **How have you seen these things happen in your life?**

11. APPLY: With these themes in mind, what would you say to someone who thinks that Christianity is a rather boring religion of "dos and don'ts"? First, the true Christian message never simply preaches a list of dos and don'ts because we can never be saved by righteous things that we have done (v 5). The Christian message is much worse news (v 3) and much better news (v 4-7) than that. A Christian has come to understand that, in the past…
- they deserved God's punishment but now they have received God's kindness, love and mercy.
- they messed up their life with selfish, hateful, rebellious sins, but now they have been given a clean new start.
- they were guilty of sin but now they have been justified.
- they were headed for death and judgment, but now they can look forward to eternal life.
So ask this person:
…What do you deserve from God?
…How much good have you achieved in your life?
…What wrong things are you guilty of and what can you do about it?
…What is your future destiny at the end of your life here on earth?

For every question, the true Christian has a better, more joyful and confident answer.

- **How would you respond to someone who, while accepting that you are a Christian, also tells you that you have not yet received the Spirit, and who claims to be able to give you the Spirit?** It is clear from 1 Cor 12 v 13 that all Christians have been baptised with the Spirit (see Session Three). From Titus 3 v 4-7 it is clear that all Christians are saved by the pouring out of the Spirit. From the descriptions in Acts of situations where the Spirit is given, it is clear that this happens when people respond in repentance and faith to the message of Jesus Christ. If you have repented and turned to Jesus Christ for the forgiveness of your sins, you can be confident that you have been baptised with the Spirit / received the gift of the Spirit and that someone who says otherwise is wrong.

12. How do these words of Jesus fit with what we have read in Acts?
According to these words of Jesus, to be born of the Spirit is to become a member of the kingdom of God, which is to become a Christian. Similarly, in the book of Acts, we have seen that when the Spirit is given, people repent and are baptised, which means that they become a Christian. To be born again of the Spirit = to receive the gift/baptism/outpouring of the Spirit = to become a Christian.

13. APPLY: Why are the following statements inadequate or wrong? "I am a Christian because…
- **I have been baptised."** Baptism should be an outward sign of an inner change— "the washing of rebirth and renewal by the Holy Spirit" (Titus 3 v 5). Without this, baptism with water is meaningless.

- **someone laid hands on me and I spoke in tongues."** As we have seen in Acts, the gift of the Spirit always resulted in repentance and turning to Jesus Christ for forgiveness. Jesus expressed the same event as being born again of the Spirit. Whatever experiences someone may have, if they do not understand who Jesus is, if they have not repented and turned to Him as Lord, they have not received the gift of the Spirit and cannot be a Christian.

- **I believe that Jesus is the Son of God."** Many people have reached the point of an intellectual acceptance of the truth about Jesus' identity, but if there is no evidence of the work of the Spirit in their lives, (ie: repentance and change to a new life with Jesus as Lord), they are not a Christian.

5 Romans 8 v 12-17; Galatians 5 v 16-26
LED BY THE SPIRIT

THE BIG IDEA
To be led by the Spirit means to be enabled to live the Christian life, doing battle with sin in this world, knowing something of the suffering of Christ in our bodies, as we struggle forward to a glorious eternal future; it doesn't mean divine guidance for specific individuals in their personal career and lifestyle decisions.

SUMMARY

The aim of this session is to show what the Bible means by the phrase "led by the Spirit"—something very different from what Christians often imagine. The popular idea of what it means to be led by the Spirit has meant that He has come to be viewed by many as a sort of divine lifestyle guru or careers advisor. Closely connected to this misunderstanding is the idea that a Christian can only find true peace and fulfilment in life when they discover how the Spirit is leading them in their personal circumstances. According to this thinking, problems and difficulties arise because someone is not being led by the Spirit. In fact, we shall see that problems and difficulties are precisely what the Spirit leads God's people into!

This session begins by looking at some of the numerous references to being "led by God" that occur in the Old Testament, before examining the four New Testament references to being "led by the Spirit". The Bible passages investigated seek to establish the following points:

- Overwhelmingly, Old Testament references to being "led by God" come from the story of the exodus and refer to God's people being led out of Egypt, through the Red Sea, through the desert and into the promised land.
- The two New Testament references about Jesus show that He was led by the Spirit, after His baptism, into the desert, where He was tempted by the devil but successfully resisted all the temptations.
- A parallel of Jesus' temptation with the exodus shows that God's people in the Old Testament failed the test in the desert by grumbling and rebelling against God, whereas God's chosen servant, Jesus Christ, passed the test, proving that He was without sin and therefore qualified

to bear our sin on the cross and give Christians His righteousness.

- The two New Testament Bible passages about Christians show that to be led by the Spirit is the opposite of living according to the flesh (sinful nature, NIV84). But more than that, when we are led by the Spirit we live in conflict with our sinful nature. The Spirit leads Christians into conflict and struggle with the sinful nature, and this equates with the experiences of both Israel and Jesus when they were led by the Spirit into the desert.
- To be led by the Spirit means to live the Christian life, which in this world is one of struggle and hardship, but in which we also have the blessing of knowing God as our Father and the hope of eternal life.

GUIDANCE FOR QUESTIONS

1. What do people usually mean when they say that they have been "led by the Spirit" or "led by God"? What is the difference between a strong desire and God's "leading"? Most people believe that God leads them, in various ways, to make the decision that He would like them to make with regard to personal choices such as careers or vocations, marriage partners, ministry, churches and lifestyle choices. People often believe that they are led by the Spirit when they have a strong desire or recurring thought that appears to be confirmed by signs such as "out of the blue" comments from other Christians or a Bible verse that seems to recommend a particular course of action. Of course, there may be nothing wrong with a strong desire, but this session will show that being "led by the Spirit" is something very different.

2. Look up the following verses and answer the questions given in the table. See table at top of next page.

	Who was leading?	Who was being led?	Where were they being led?
Ex 13 v 17-18	God	Israel	through the desert
Psalm 106 v 9	God	Israel	through the Red Sea
Ezekiel 20 v 10	God	Israel	out of Egypt and into the desert
Deut 8 v 2, 15	God	Israel	through the desert and its many dangers (v15)
Nehemiah 9 v 12	God (v 7)	Israel	through the desert
Judges 2 v 1	Angel of the LORD (God)	Israel	out of Egypt and into the promised land

All of these Old Testament references to being led by God are about the exodus—when God, by His mighty acts and under the leadership of His chosen servant, Moses, rescued His people from Egypt and took them through the desert into the promised land. We can conclude that "led by God" in the Old Testament refers to the whole people of God (Israel), who are led in keeping with His great plan and promises to Abraham—it doesn't refer to individuals who are led according to a personalised plan of God for their lives.

See also Psalm 78 v 13, 52; Psalm 136 v 16; Isaiah 48 v 21; Isaiah 63 v 13; Jeremiah 2 v 17; Hosea 11 v 4; Amos 2 v 10; Acts 7 v 36; Acts 13 v 17. In the Old Testament the phrase "led by God" is overwhelmingly used to refer to the exodus. There are a few references to Abraham, but that is also about being led to the promised land.

3. APPLY: If an Old Testament Israelite in the desert had said: "I feel God is leading me to go back to Egypt and start a melon farm", how would you have answered him? You could be confident that this was not God's leading since in the Old Testament, God led His

people only in accordance with His great master plan. This was to take them out of Egypt, through the desert to the land that He had promised long before to Abraham, where they would become a nation that would bring God's blessing to the whole world. Since God was already leading His people away from Egypt, an individual's wish to return to Egypt could not be the result of God's leading.

4. What similarities are there with the exodus? Both Israel and Jesus were led into the desert. Both passed through a baptism before going into the desert—Israel through the Red Sea and Jesus baptised by John in the Jordan River. Israel spent 40 years in the desert and Jesus 40 days. Both went through difficult experiences there. **What differences are there (compare Hebrews 3 v 7-8 and 4 v 15)?** Israel failed the test and responded to hardship by grumbling and rebelling against God (Hebrews 3 v 7-8). Jesus passed the test and was found to be without sin despite being tempted in every way, just as we are (Hebrews 4 v 15).

5. Where did the Spirit lead Jesus? Why? The Spirit led Jesus into the desert to be tempted so that, in resisting all temptation, Jesus could be proved to be without sin, and so qualified both to bear our sin on the cross and give Christians His righteousness (see 2 Corinthians 5 v 21).

6. Both of these passages show us two ways to live. In the table below list everything that you learn from these verses about the two ways to live. See table below.

Note: "If you are led by the Spirit, you are not under law" (Galatians 5 v 18). To understand what this means you need to refer back to Galatians 4 v 21-30, where Paul, who is writing to Christians wanting to go back to following Jewish laws, uses the Old Testament stories of Sarah and Hagar, (wife and concubine respectively of Abraham), to illustrate the difference between God's old and new covenants with His people. Hagar, whose children became slaves, illustrates the old covenant given at Sinai—God's people had to obey His law, and if they failed to do so, which was always the case, they would be judged by it. Paul points out that this is the slavery that the Galatian Christians want to return to—they want to put themselves again "under law". Sarah, who miraculously gave birth to the child of promise, illustrates the new covenant—God's people are now those who

Flesh (sinful nature)	Spirit
Romans 8 v 12-17 • You will die (v 13) • You are slaves to fear (v 15)	Romans 8 v 12-17 • You put to death the misdeeds of the body (v 13) • You will live (v 13) • You become children of God (v 14, 15, 16) • You become heirs of God and co-heirs with Christ (v 17) • You share in Christ's suffering (v 17) • You will share in Christ's glory (v 17)
Galatians 5 v 16-26 • You are in conflict with the Spirit (v 17) • You participate in the acts of the sinful nature: sexual immorality, impurity and debauchery, idolatry and witchcraft, hatred, discord, jealousy, fits of rage, selfish ambition, dissensions, factions, envy, drunkenness, orgies etc. (v 19-21) • You will not inherit the kingdom of God (v 21)	Galatians 5 v 16-26 • You will not gratify the desires of the flesh (v 16) • You are in conflict with the flesh (v 17) • You are not under the law (v 18—see note below for Q6) • You produce the fruit of the Spirit: love, joy, peace, forbearance, kindness, goodness faithfulness and self-control (v 22) • You have crucified the flesh with its passions and desires (v 24) • You can and should keep in step with the Spirit (v 25)

have been given the miracle of new birth by the Spirit. Ezekiel expressed this as having the law written on their hearts, rather than imposed externally as at Sinai. They are "led by the Spirit" and so they are "not under law".

7. Look at both passages. Who is being led by the Spirit?
Romans 8: Christians—those who "belong to Christ" (see v 9).
Galatians 5: Christians—"those who belong to Christ" (v 24).

8. Look at Romans 8 v 12-17. Where are these people led to?
- v 13: struggle ("put to death the misdeeds of the body")
- v 13: life
- v 14: sonship ("sons of God")
- v 17: suffering
- v 17: glory

9. What does it mean to be "led by the Spirit"? To be "led by the Spirit" means to live the Christian life, experiencing both its hardships (the struggle with sin and suffering) and its blessings (the privilege of being children of God and the hope of eternal life and glory).

10. APPLY: From what we have learned about being led by the Spirit, what should we expect the Christian life to be like? One of both difficulty and blessing, struggle and joy, battle and peace. The Old Testament parallel with the life of the Christian in this world is the 40 years when Israel wandered in the desert. Although now is the time of struggle and suffering, temptation and testing, we also have the joyful hope of eternal glory, and the presence of the Spirit is leading us there. It is the emphasis on the difficulty of the Christian life now that will surprise many, particularly in the context of being led by the Spirit. This is because many have misunderstood the term "led by the Spirit" and, wrongly used to describe personal guidance, it has become associated with ideas of fulfilment.

- **How could you help a Christian who says: "I'm not doing very well. The Christian life is such a struggle for me. I'm always battling with a particular sin."** Battling with sin is evidence that this person is being led by the Spirit, and therefore, as we shall see in Session Eight, that they are a son of God. It is the Christian who is not battling that is not doing very well.

11. Look at Galatians 5 v 25. What command is given to those who are born again ("live"—NIV) by the Spirit? What does that mean? Those who "live by the Spirit" (are born again) are commanded to "keep in step with the Spirit" (other versions—"walk by the Spirit"). That means living in obedience to what the Spirit wants.

12. How does Galatians 5 v 17 describe the reality of what it means to keep in step with the Spirit? Compare this with what we have learned from Romans 8 and the experience of Jesus when He was led by the Spirit. If we keep in step with the Spirit, we will have to do what is contrary to the sinful nature; this will mean a battle. Similarly, Romans 8 v 13 talks about putting to death the misdeeds of the body—clearly a painful process. In the same way, Jesus suffered when He was tempted in the desert because He chose to do what was harder, in obedience to God, rather than to take the easy way out, suggested by the devil.

13. Why is walking such a good picture for living the Christian life? Walking involves activity and effort—we are not simply waiting around for eternal life, but are involved in a daily battle with our own sinful nature, with temptation and with suffering. The fact that we are walking indicates that we haven't yet reached our destination—our hope should be set on future glory rather than finding satisfaction in this world.

14. APPLY: Can you be a Christian, but not be led by the Spirit? If you are not led by the Spirit you cannot be a Christian. In the same way that God led Israel out of Egypt and through the desert to the promised land, Christians are those who have been rescued by Jesus Christ from slavery to sin and death, are now living a life of struggle against sin in this world, and are on their way to eternal life.

• **Can you be a Christian, but not walk by the Spirit?** Sometimes Christians give in to their sinful nature and fail to do what God wants. They are led by the Spirit but they are not keeping in step with Him.

6 Ephesains 5 v 15-22
FILLED WITH THE SPIRIT

THE BIG IDEA
To be filled with the Spirit has different meanings, depending on which New Testament writer uses the term and its biblical context—it means living the Christian life in the community of the church, as explained by Paul in Ephesians 5, or being empowered to carry out the task of prophesying, preaching and witnessing, as used by Luke.

SUMMARY
Many people understand the term "filled with the Spirit" to mean an overwhelming experience of spiritual joy or power that comes upon a person, sometimes in answer to prayer, and sometimes unsought. This experience may enable a person to do unusual or supernatural things such as speaking with divine authority, healing, casting out evil spirits, giving an insight or prophecy about a situation etc. Or it may simply give the individual a deeper appreciation of God's love, greater faith and trust in God, increased joy or love for others etc. People who regularly receive such experiences come to be known as "Spirit-filled Christians", and a ministry characterised by these kinds of phenomena is termed a "Spirit-filled ministry". However, a survey of the way in which "filled with the Spirit" is used in the New Testament shows something different. In the New Testament, two writers use the term "filled with the Spirit"—Luke and Paul—and by looking at the context of this phrase we can see that each writer means something different.

Luke: Luke comes nearest to today's popular view of being filled with the Spirit, yet there are significant differences. According to Luke, the purpose for which Christians are filled with the Spirit is for proclaiming and defending God's word, the gospel of Jesus Christ. To begin with, in Luke's Gospel, he uses the term "filled with the Spirit" in an Old Testament way (see Session Two)—the Holy Spirit comes upon specially chosen individuals (John the Baptist, Elizabeth and Zechariah) for a special purpose (to prophesy about the coming of God's Saviour). But then, in Acts, Luke comes to Pentecost, the fulfilment of Joel's prophecy that all God's servants would receive the Spirit and prophesy. From then on, "filled with the Spirit" refers to the apostles/believers/disciples or individual Christians (Peter and Saul/Paul), always for the purpose of proclaiming or defending the Christian message, and often in the context of opposition or persecution.

Luke's writings are descriptions of events in the early church, rather than explanations of what it is to be and live as a Christian; so we need to be careful about applying the experiences of these first believers directly to ourselves. However, we know from Acts 1 v 5 that the grand purpose in Jesus pouring out the Spirit was that ultimately, Jesus' followers would be His witnesses to the ends of the earth—something that was clearly not fulfilled by the end of the book of Acts. Christians today are continuing to take the gospel to the ends of the earth. There seems to be no reason why God wouldn't fill Christians with the Spirit in the same way today, and for the same purpose—to help His people to be bold in proclaiming and defending the message of Jesus, especially in the face of opposition and persecution.

Note: Luke also uses a related term "full of the Spirit", which sometimes means the same as "filled with the Spirit", but sometimes refers to godly character. For a survey of verses in Luke's writing that refer to "full of the Spirit", see optional extra at the end of the session.

Paul: When Paul writes "be filled with the Spirit" (Ephesians 5 v 18), he is giving Christians an instruction in a letter that explains what it means to be a Christian, and how a Christian should live. So this instruction is clearly also meant for Christians today. But Paul's use of "filled with the Spirit" is very different from the popular idea outlined above. What Paul means by "filled with the Spirit" is living a godly life in the context of the Christian community—the church. The fact that he gives an instruction or command to be filled with the Spirit also shows that it is not an experience but an action.

When looking at Ephesians 5 v 18-21 it is important that people understand that Paul has written, not five separate commands (be filled with the Spirit, speak…, sing…, give thanks…, submit…), but one command that is expressed in four ways, using an "ing" word (be filled with the Spirit… speaking… singing… giving thanks… and submitting). In other words, the way to be filled with the Spirit is to do these four things. It may be helpful to have another version available (eg: ESV), in which the English translation follows more closely the grammar of the original Greek, which was written as one sentence.

GUIDANCE FOR QUESTIONS

1. Have you ever been drunk? How does drunkenness transform a person? The key point is that when drunk, a person can be completely transformed, even to the extent of becoming like someone we don't know, or behaving in a way which we never thought them capable of. This is the point we will return to when we consider the analogy between being drunk on wine and being filled with the Spirit in Q8 below.

2. Scan the whole of Ephesians 5. What is the main theme of this passage? If you scan Ephesians 5, you will see that Paul is talking about living a godly life eg: "Be imitators of God" (v 1). This is particularly in the context of the church, the Christian community; notice how many of the instructions in this passage involve relationships with others. By the time we get to verse 15, it's obvious what the main theme of the passage is. What is not obvious, especially in the NIV, is the fact that in the original Greek, verses 15-22 are written as one sentence. By the time we come to verse 18, we are in mid-flow of a sentence that is all about holiness.

3. Fill in the blanks. Two commands (v 18):
Don't get drunk on wine
Do be filled with the Spirit
The reason (v 16): the days are evil.
Therefore (v 17): do not be foolish but understand what the Lord's will is
And (v 18) be filled with the Spirit.

4. What are the four actions that show someone is filled with the Spirit (v 19-21)? The four resulting actions of being filled with the Spirit are:
- speaking to one another with psalms, hymn and spiritual songs;
- singing and making music in your heart to the Lord;
- always giving thanks to God the Father for everything, in the name of Jesus;
- submitting to one another out of reverence for Christ.

5. What do these four things have in common? These are not things that we would naturally do. All of these four actions focus away from ourselves towards God and towards others.

- **Why does Paul call them "being filled with the Spirit", do you think?** The Spirit helps us to please God. We cannot do this without the Spirit (Romans 8 v 8).

6. Would it be correct to describe being filled with the Spirit as an experience? Why or why not? While people may experience things such as joy or peace or understanding when they are filled with the Spirit, because they are living as God designed them to, it is clear from these verses that Paul is not primarily talking about experiences but about godly activity. Each of these marks of the filling of the Spirit results in a person doing something or relating to someone in a godly way—it leads to a change in behaviour. Paul can't command an experience—he commands actions.

7. According to the passage, how is getting drunk on wine different to being filled with the Spirit? It leads to debauchery (v 18) ie: uncontrolled and self-seeking indulgence. Getting filled with the Spirit leads to a right relationship with God and others, expressed in submission, self-control etc.

8. How is getting drunk on wine similar to being filled with the Spirit? What is the point of the comparison? Getting drunk on wine and being filled with the Spirit are similar in that both lead to a dramatic change of behaviour. The point of the comparison is that when we are controlled by something or someone else, we should make sure that we are controlled for godly and selfless purposes (ie: by the Spirit), not for destructive and selfish purposes. People commonly misunderstand the point of this comparison—they equate being filled with the Spirit with ecstatic experiences that look like drunkenness (falling down, uncontrollable laughter or weeping etc.). But according to Paul, being filled with the Spirit shows itself in behaviour that is completely opposite to these passive, self-fulfilling experiences—it shows itself in self-controlled and selfless action that seeks to glorify God and to serve others.

9. What does [Col 3 v 16-17] mention instead [of being filled with the Spirit]? What conclusions can we draw from this? It instructs us to be filled with the word of Christ. When taken as a parallel of Ephesians 5 v 18-20, this verse occupies the place of Paul's instruction to be filled with the Spirit. We have already seen the close link between God's word and God's Spirit in Session One. The implication is that if we let the word of Christ dwell in us richly, we shall be filled with the Spirit—and that if we are filled with the Spirit, the word of Christ will dwell in us richly.

10. APPLY: How can we tell whether someone is truly filled with the Spirit? From what we have learned in this session, we can see that those who are filled with the Spirit will act to glorify God and serve others in the Christian faith, in the ways outlined by Paul in Ephesians 5 v 19-20. Towards God, they will have an attitude of joy, expressed in singing and making music in their hearts, and they will be people who give thanks for everything in the name of the Lord Jesus Christ. Towards others, they will have an attitude of serving by speaking God's truth, not as public speakers and teachers, but by using psalms, hymns and spiritual songs to encourage and challenge one another. Their relationships will be marked by submission to one another. **Note:** These marks of being filled with the Spirit are very different to what many imagine when they hear the term "Spirit-filled".

- **Notice that Ephesians 5 v 18 gives us a command. How can we obey it?** The fact that verses 18-20 are a single sentence in the original Greek indicates that we are actually filled with the Spirit when we do the actions listed here by Paul—that is what being filled with the Spirit is. The Spirit is not some kind of divine inspiration that comes to us independently of how we live and act, nor do we pray to be filled with Him and then passively wait for some experience or spectacular event to occur. If you are speaking God's truth to others, singing to the Lord, giving thanks to Him for everything in the name of Jesus, and submitting to others out of reverence for Christ… you are following the command to be filled with the Spirit. This is very similar to walking (keeping in step) with the Spirit (Galatians 5 v 25)—by the Spirit we walk, but we walk.

11. Look up the following verses and answer the questions given in the table. See table at top of next page.

12. What is the difference between the way in which Luke uses the term "filled with the Spirit", and the way Paul uses it in Ephesians 5? Luke doesn't use "filled with the Spirit" to refer to being a godly person, but rather, to describe a special empowering at a special time for a particular purpose. The purpose is always connected with speaking God's word, often in the context of opposition or persecution. On several occasions the filling of the Spirit gives the Christians courage to speak.

- **Complete the following sentences: In Luke's writing, in contrast to Paul's, being filled with the Spirit is not…** godly living in the Christian community (the church).

	Who is filled with the Spirit?	For what purpose?
Luke 1 v 15	John the Baptist	v 16-17 To prophesy to Israel and prepare people for the Lord
Luke 1 v 41	Elizabeth	v 42-45 To prophesy about Mary and the baby she was carrying
Luke 1 v 67	Zechariah	v 68-79 To prophesy about God's salvation
Acts 2 v 4	The apostles	v 4, 11 To declare the wonders of God in many tongues
Acts 4 v 8	Peter	v 8-12 To preach the message of Jesus Christ
Acts 4 v 31	The believers	To speak the word of God boldly
Acts 9 v 17	Saul/Paul	v 15 To take the gospel to the Gentiles
Acts 13 v 9	Saul/Paul	v 10-11 To prophesy against Elymas the sorcerer
Acts 13 v 52	The disciples	v 49-51 To persevere in preaching the gospel after rejection in Antioch

It is ... being empowered by the Spirit for the purpose of speaking God's word boldly, especially in situations of opposition and persecution.

13. APPLY: What would you expect to see in someone who is filled with the Spirit, according to Luke's use of the term? You would expect to see them proclaiming the gospel boldly.

• **How should this encourage us in the task of evangelism?** Most people find evangelism scary. Why not take time to discuss with your group how this session can encourage us in the task of evangelism?

OPTIONAL EXTRA

To see more about what Luke means by "full of the Spirit", look up Luke 4 v 1; 10 v 21; Acts 6 v 3; 6 v 5; 7 v 55; 11 v 24. For each, ask and answer the following questions:
• Who is full of the Spirit?
• Is this the same as Luke's use of "filled with the Spirit", or different?
• If the same, for what purpose or reason?
• Are they filled with anything else?

7 1 Corinthians 12 v 4-31
GIFTS OF THE SPIRIT

THE BIG IDEA
The gifts of the Spirit are gifts to the church, rather than to individual Christians, for the purpose of building up the church.

SUMMARY
The aim of this session is to help people have a truly biblical understanding of gifts of the Spirit, by examining the five lists of gifts in the New Testament and the context in which they are given. The session focuses particularly on 1 Corinthians 12. When people don't understand the New Testament teaching on gifts of the Spirit, it can lead to problems and errors such as:

- Christians who don't believe that they have a gift.
- Christians who don't know what their gift is, and don't know how to discover it.
- churches that expect everyone to be the same.
- the tendency to equate gifts of the Spirit with natural abilities.
- the belief that all gifts of the Spirit are miraculous.
- the belief that all the gifts of the Spirit are listed in the NT, and there are no others.
- the tendency to ignore the purpose for which gifts of the Spirit are given ie: the common good.
- people who view their gift as a means of self-expression and personal fulfilment.
- the belief that all gifts (as opposed to people) are equal.

The Bible passages investigated seek to establish the following points:
- Gifts of the Spirit are given for the common good of the body of Christ.
- The common good = building up the church to unity in faith and knowledge, and maturity.
- Use of these gifts involves administering God's grace to one another; using your ability to serve your own interest is not a gift of the Spirit.
- There are many different kinds of gifts and it seems that the New Testament does not comprehensively list them all.
- Not all gifts are miraculous.
- All believers receive a gift or gifts of the Spirit and all have a part to play in the body of Christ.
- There are greater gifts that are all to do with ministry of God's word.
- The greater gifts should be eagerly desired by the church, not by individuals.

GUIDANCE FOR QUESTIONS
1. Think of ways in which Christians are encouraged/advised to discover the gift that each of them has. What is good or bad about these methods? Often people are encouraged to make a list of activities or skills that they enjoy and/or are good at. But:

a. this suggests that a natural ability is the same thing as a spiritual gift.

b. what happens if you don't feel that you are good at anything?

c. what happens if you are self-deluded and wrongly believe that you are good at something?

d. this method completely ignores the fact that you are part of a community, the church, who have no say in the matter.

e. this method will lead people to focus on personal satisfaction and self-promotion. As we shall see, the NT has a very different approach to gifts of the Spirit.

Another suggestion may be that you ask other Christians or leaders what they think your gift might be. This is a healthier approach in that it includes the church in recognising gifts of the Spirit.

2. Look up the verses in the table … (all are related to the five lists mentioned above) and note down the word or phrase that is used to describe "gifts of the Spirit".

1 Cor 12 v 4	gift
v 5	service
v 6	working
v 7	manifestation of the Spirit
v 11	work of the Spirit
1 Cor 14 v 1	gifts of the Spirit
Rom 12 v 6	gifts according to the grace given us
Eph 4 v 7	grace given as Christ apportioned it
1 Peter 4 v 10	gift

- **What can we learn about the gifts of the Spirit from the words used to describe them?**
  - spiritual / of the Spirit: gifts to further the Spirit's work, not promote our success, prosperity, influence etc.
  - according to grace: these gifts are given by God undeservedly—we cannot boast in them (either individually or as churches) and we should be thankful to God for them.
  - service/working/work of the Spirit: these gifts are about serving one another, not promoting ourselves; and about work, not just personal

enjoyment or fulfilment.

3. Write down all the gifts that are mentioned in the five lists.

1 Cor 12 v 8-10	the message of wisdom; the message of knowledge; faith; gifts of healing; miraculous powers; prophecy; distinguishing between spirits; speaking in tongues; interpreting tongues
1 Cor 12 v 28-30	apostles; prophets; teachers; workers of miracles; gifts of healing; ability to help others; guidance/administration; speaking in tongues
Rom 12 v 6-8	prophesying; serving; teaching; encouraging; giving; leadership; showing mercy
Eph 4 v 11	apostles; prophets; evangelists; pastors and teachers
1 Peter 4 v 11	speaking; serving

Note: There is also a reference to gifts of the Spirit in Hebrews 2 v 4, but, as it does not specify what the gifts are, it has not been included in the table.

4. What can we learn about gifts of the Spirit from comparing the five lists?
There are many different kinds of gifts ranging from the miraculous (workers of miracles) and prominent (apostles) to the supportive (encouraging) and apparently mundane (administration).

- **What proportion of the gifts listed would you describe as miraculous?**
  It is not exactly certain what some gifts described in 1 Cor were (eg: distinguishing between spirits). However, it is clear that only some gifts in some lists could be described as miraculous, while three

of the lists contain no miraculous gifts at all. (Rom 12 v 6-8, Eph 4 v 11 and 1 Peter 4 v 11). It may be significant that all the miraculous gifts are found in the lists from 1 Corinthians. The Corinthian church was plagued with false notions of spirituality based on worldly wisdom, eloquence, special knowledge, asceticism and spectacular supernatural phenomena, that had led them to reject the authority of apostles like Paul, and to drift into all kinds of error. As Paul sought to rebuild relationships with this church, it may be that he was deliberately choosing examples of what they considered to be gifts of the Spirit, as he corrected and explained to them what gifts were really about. Whatever the reason, miraculous gifts of the Spirit are not mentioned in any other list of gifts.

- **Do you think that the table in Q3 represents a complete list of all gifts of the Spirit? If yes, why are the lists different?** None of the lists contain all of the gifts of the Spirit that are mentioned in the New Testament. If the five lists together constitute the entire range of gifts available, why is it that they are never mentioned all at once? Note that Paul uses the phrase "gift from God" when talking about singleness (1 Corinthians 7 v 7), but none of the five lists mention singleness as a gift of the Spirit. It seems more likely that each time a New Testament writer wanted to talk about gifts of the Spirit, he selected examples of some gifts. In that case, there are many more gifts of the Spirit than have been mentioned in the five lists.

5. What can we learn from Peter's concise list? It seems to be a summary of the functions of all the gifts of the Spirit.

6. What are the main themes of this passage [ie: 1 Cor 12 v 12-26]? Oneness and interdependence.

7. In what way are all Christians the same? All God's people have been baptised by the one Spirit and are part of one body, all have the Spirit working through them and all have a part to play in the functioning of the body.

8. In what way are Christians different? Each Christian has a different part to play in the functioning of the body.

9. Why is the body such a wonderful illustration of the church? A body is a wonderfully designed and complex organism, in which many very different parts all work together under the command of the head. From experience, we know how much the whole body is affected when even one tiny part of the body malfunctions (eg: an ingrown toenail). So the body is an accurate illustration of the sheer variety of people that should be found in the church, their individual importance, their utter interdependence and their profound unity, unmatched by any human organisation.

10. Do all gifts have the same, or different purposes? What is the purpose of gifts of the Spirit (v 7)? The body illustration suggests that all the gifts have one purpose, just as all the parts of the body work together for the well-being of the whole body. Verse 7 tells us that each Christian is given a manifestation or gift of the Spirit "for the common good".

11. What is the common good? Anything that meets the needs and promotes the well-being of the church. **How is the purpose of the gifts described in Ephesians 4**

v 12-13 and 1 Peter 4 v 10?
- **Ephesians 4 v 12-13:** The purpose of the gifts is "to equip [God's] people for works of service, so that the body of Christ may be built up" to unity in faith and knowledge, and maturity.
- **1 Peter 4 v 10:** We should use our gifts "to serve others, as faithful stewards of God's grace in its various forms".
- **What does 1 Corinthians 13 v 1-3 add?** Without love, our gifts are useless and worthless.

12. APPLY: Look at the following statements and discuss whether they are right or wrong.
- **"A gift is not given to me for my good; it is given to the church."** Right—the Spirit gives gifts for the common good of God's people, not for my own personal fulfilment or satisfaction (although, of course, the common good includes my good as well).
- **"I love church because it gives me the opportunity to express myself by using my gift."** Wrong—this is a very harmful and dangerous attitude. This person is not thinking at all about serving others, and will only act to serve their own interests. So, whatever ability they may have, it cannot be described as a gift of the Spirit. A person who thinks like this is likely to end up causing problems in the church or leaving, if they believe that they are not being given an opportunity to express themselves.
- **"The church has 15 good piano-players, but I want my turn, because piano-playing is my gift."** Wrong—similar to above. Instead of waiting around uselessly to do a job that has already been oversubscribed, this person should be asking about or looking for other needs in

the church that they could meet.
- **"The church needs someone to put out chairs before the meeting. I'm available and able to do this. Is this my gift?"** Right—this is a great way to discover your gift. It doesn't mean that you stick at this one job for ever. The needs of a church will change constantly as people come and go and another need may come up for which only you are able and equipped to help.
- **"To discover what my gift is, I'm going to work out what I enjoy and what I'm good at, and offer that to the church."** Wrong—again the emphasis is on my interests, and there is no mention of what the church might need.
- **"God used me in my previous church in a number of ways. In my new church I'm just offering my help wherever I can."** Right—since gifts of the Spirit are given for the common good, there is no reason why a person wouldn't exercise a different gift when they move to a new church, where the needs may be different. Similarly, an old gift might become redundant. Your previous church may be full of affluent people who give generously, but as they are all creative types, there is a desperate need for someone to do administration. Your new church may have a number of people who are willing to serve with admin. But people are either hard-up or unwilling to give, so there isn't much money available for gospel work. If you have a reasonable income, it may be that your gift will change to that of giving.

Note: There are some gifts that every church will always need (see Q13 to 15. In this case, it would be wrong for a church to keep someone who had been given one of these greater gifts in a situation where they never use that gift. If a church is already chock-full of teachers, they shouldn't hold on to someone who is gifted at teaching, and only use them for administration or practical help (see Acts 6 v 1-4). There is the common good of the whole church to consider. (If people raise this issue at this point, it would be best to ask them to wait until questions 13 to 15 have been discussed.)

13. What are the greater gifts [1 Cor 12 v 28-31]? The greater gifts are those that Paul ranks in verse 28—apostles, prophets and teachers. **What do these gifts have in common?** They are all concerned with speaking God's word. **What is the role of people who have these gifts (see also Acts 6 v 1-4)?** To bring God's word to people. Acts 6 v 1-4 shows that the ministry of God's word and the responsibility of praying for God's people were considered so important by the apostles that no other need, however urgent, was permitted to distract them from this work.
Note: The apostles were men who had met with the risen Jesus, and were chosen by Him for this role. Prophets here refers to people who are gifted to open up God's word and apply it today to people's lives and the church.

14. Why are the "greater gifts" greater? Compare 1 Cor 14 v 1-5. Because they build up God's people with His word. They are about that which all the other gifts are serving eg: an administrator organises a church meeting so that the church can hear the word of God preached by a gifted preacher. Someone puts the chairs out because it helps people to hear the teaching of the word of God. Therefore, the gift of putting out chairs is not inferior or something to be despised—it serves the church by helping them to hear the word of God, which builds them up.

15. Look at 1 Cor 12 v 31. If Christians all have different gifts, how is it that we should all equally desire the greater gifts? If we believe that the Spirit gives gifts to individuals, this instruction is difficult to understand, since in the previous verses Paul has been at pains to teach that each Christian has different gifts and roles in the body. The instruction to eagerly desire the greater gifts only makes sense when we understand that the Spirit gives gifts to the church for the common good. Each Christian should eagerly desire to see the greater gifts at work in their church, and in the worldwide church. **How can we desire the greater gifts?** By praying for them, supporting those who already exercise these gifts, doing everything we can to encourage and make possible the training of future prophets and teachers, and making sure that the ministry of God's word and prayer have the most important place in all our church activities.

16. APPLY: What does a church look like when the Spirit is at work?
- The Christians are united.
- Diversity is permitted—there are Christians of different class, race, age and personality equally contributing to the common good.
- The church is being built up to unity in faith and knowledge, and maturity.
- People are serving one another.
- People are flexible about their roles and willing to do what is necessary to meet the needs of the moment.
- There is a central role for the ministry of God's word and prayer.
- Teachers and prophets are freed from other distractions to use those gifts.

8 Romans 8 v 1-39
THE SPIRIT AND YOU

THE BIG IDEA

In Christ Jesus, with the Spirit at work in us and for us, whatever our situation of suffering or persecution, we can be sure that nothing will ever be able to condemn us and separate us from the love of God.

SUMMARY

Romans 8 contains more references to the Spirit than any other chapter in the Bible. Yet this passage is all about the work and achievements of Jesus Christ (v 1-4, 9-11, 17, 29-30, 32-35, 39). This shouldn't surprise us, as we have already seen that the work of the Spirit is to glorify Christ. In fact, a number of the things that we look at in this session have already been investigated in previous Bible studies. But this is a great opportunity to review these truths and see what a difference they make for people who are really suffering or struggling.

Suffering, persecution, slanderous accusations, weakness, failing bodies—these are the things that have always caused Christians to doubt whether God loves them, and to feel abandoned or condemned by Him. Paul wrote into this situation to fire us up with utter confidence in God's unshakeable love for us, not because we are strong, but because of what Christ has done for us, what the Spirit does for us, who God is and what He will do for us.

This session is not sufficient to investigate and discover all the treasures that this remarkable passage contains. But the aim is to give opportunity for Christians to reflect on and revel in the tremendous truth of what it means to be "in Christ", "led by the Spirit" and "sons of God".

The main points of this session are:
- There is now no condemnation for those who are in Christ.
- In Christ we are set free from the force within us that causes us to sin, by the greater power of the Spirit.
- God's law is powerless to help us—it can only condemn us.
- Jesus removed the condemnation of God's law by suffering it in Himself, as a sin-offering.
- The Spirit-controlled person sets their mind on what the Spirit desires.
- Because the Spirit lives in us we can be confident that our bodies will be resurrected in the future.
- The Spirit convinces us that we are children of God.
- Although we suffer now we will share in Christ's glory.
- Whatever our situations of suffering or persecution, we can be sure that nothing will separate us from the love of God.

Note: Romans 8 v 2—"The law of sin and death"—doesn't mean God's law. It is the force at work in us that causes us to break God's law (sin) and so earns His just penalty (death). However, the two types of "law" are closely related in that the force of sin in us is only revealed to us by the law of God.

GUIDANCE FOR QUESTIONS

1. What sort of things can bring a Christian (someone whose sins have been forgiven because of Jesus) under a sense of condemnation, or fear that God no longer loves them? Christians can be led by adverse experiences in this world—temptation and sin, sickness, ageing, death, disappointments and frustrations, persecution and suffering—to believe that God is punishing them and no longer loves them. This session will show that the antidote to this kind of problem is confidence in and reliance on the saving work of Jesus Christ, outlined in v 1-4.

2. What is Paul's big theme in this passage (see verses 1, 33-34 and 38-39)?
The tremendous news that there is "now no condemnation for those who are in Christ Jesus" (v 1). By "no condemnation" Paul means that for the Christian, Judgment Day has already taken place—a Christian will never be judged and punished by God for their sin. The truth of verse 1 means that no one can bring any charge against God's people, since God Himself has justified them through Christ's death, and there is no one greater than God to undo His saving work (v 33-34). It also means that whatever happens in this world, nothing and no one can separate God's people from His love to us in Christ (v 38-39).
You should allow your group time to revel in this key point. What a wonderful and liberating truth this is in verse 1! We walk away from God's law court not condemned...

- no condemnation for original sin (the sinful nature that everyone has inherited from Adam);
- no condemnation for the sins committed in the past, present or future;
- no condemnation even though we fall and fail and feel condemned;
- no condemnation however much the devil accuses us;
- no condemnation whatever others say;
- no condemnation when we are physically sick or going through emotional pressures.

3. How has Jesus done what the law
of God couldn't do for us? Compare Romans 5 v 6. God's law condemns those that break the law, and the law cannot do anything to lift that condemnation from sinners (3 v 20). But Jesus was sent as a sin offering—Jesus, in the likeness of sinful man, suffered in Himself the condemnation of God on our sin, so that we would not have to suffer it ourselves.

4. How do we receive the benefit of what Jesus has done for us (v 1-4)? The
only way that we can get the benefit of what Jesus has done is to be "in Christ" (v 1). Verse 4 expresses this in a different way—living according to the Spirit, not according to the sinful nature. (The connection between being "in Christ" and "having the Spirit" is examined in questions 6 and 7 below.) **What is not the way to receive it?** Verse 3 makes it clear that we cannot be free from condemnation by following God's law—the law is powerless to help us because our sinful nature means that we can never keep the law, and therefore we are always condemned by it.

5. Paul has already told us that undeserving sinners can be made right with God through what Jesus Christ has done (3 v 22-24). Why is he again stressing that there is no condemnation for those who are "in Christ"? (See 7 v 14-25; 8 v 10, 18, 22.) When our minds and senses are battered day to day by our frailty and mortality, our flaws and sins, and our suffering, we can begin to believe that these are indications that God no longer loves or accepts us. Paul has already told us that God's love for us is shown in Christ's death on the cross (see Romans 5 v 8). That is where we should look for an answer to the question: does God still love me? But Paul himself understood the despair that

Christians can feel when, for instance, all they can think about is the sin that they can't stop doing (see 7 v 24). It is out of this kind of experience, but also because of his understanding and utter confidence in the saving power of Jesus Christ (see 7 v 25) that Paul writes Romans 8.

6. How can we know whether we are "in Christ" (8 v 9)? 8 v 9—those who have the Spirit of Christ (also referred to in the same verse as the Spirit of God living in you) belong to Christ. 8 v 10—all of these phrases are summed up in another—"Christ is in you". So "in Christ" (v 1) / "belonging to Christ" (v 9) / "Christ in you" (v 10) = "living according to the Spirit" (v 4) / "the Spirit of God living in you" (v 9) / "having the spirit of Christ" (v 9). All these phrases mean the same thing. See also 1 Cor 12 v 3.

7. How do we know we have the Spirit?

- **v 5**—our minds will be set on what the Spirit desires. Notice that this is not saying that we will always do what the Spirit desires. Paul has already described what it feels like to be someone whose mind is set on what the Spirit desires but who often doesn't or can't follow that through (see 7 v 22-24). It follows therefore that Christians will often feel at war within themselves, as Paul did. But the reason we feel disappointment, frustration and even despair at our own sinfulness is precisely because our minds are set on what the Spirit desires—compare the sinful mind, which is utterly hostile to God (v 6-8). These painful emotions are themselves a sign that we are living according to the Spirit.

- **v 13-14**—we are led by the Spirit (v 14), which means that we "put to death the misdeeds of the body" (v 13). In Session Five we saw that to be led by the Spirit is not only the opposite of living according to the flesh, but also living in conflict with the flesh.

- **v 15-16**—we no longer hide in fear from God as our Judge; we understand that He is our perfect heavenly Father. V 16—we also have an inner conviction, which is the result of the Spirit testifying with our spirit. This is not the only sign, but it is an important one. It may not be a constant sign (just as we are not constantly obedient in putting to death the misdeeds of the body), but we should experience this conviction at times in our lives.

8. Look again at verses 14-16. What is the difference between the relationship of a slave and his master, and that of a son and his father? Think about the following areas... See the table below.

	Slave/Master	Son/Father
Why obey?	Duty, fear of punishment, hope of reward	Desire to please father, love
What happens when you fail?	Cover up, run away	Seek out father to confess and be forgiven
What are your hopes for the future?	Uncertain—no security, no rights	Secure—always part of the family, an heir
What is most important to you?	To do your duty	To enjoy and grow in your relationship

9. What is the future for the children of God (v 17)? God's inheritance and Christ's glory (v 17). **What does this mean?** Everything that belongs to the Son belongs to us. God has in store for us what He has in store for Jesus—no rejects, no hand-me-downs. We are headed for glory. But we will also share in His suffering. The path to eternal life is the road of suffering. That's how it was with Christ—that's how it will be for us. "For the joy set before him [he] endured the cross" (Hebrews 12 v 2).

10. What is the contrast in verses 18-27 between now and the future? List what Paul says are the characteristics of each for the Christian. *Now:*
- Present sufferings (v 18)
- Creation frustrated (v 20)
- Bondage to decay (v 21)
- Creation groaning (v 22)
- Christians groaning, even though we have the firstfruits of the Spirit (v 23)
- Waiting eagerly and patiently, in hope (v 23 and 25)
- Weakness (v 26)
- Not knowing what to pray (v 26)
- Spirit groaning and interceding for us (v 26)

The future:
- Glory to be revealed in God's people (v 18)
- Children of God revealed (v 19)
- Liberation from decay (v 21).
- Freedom and glory for Christians (v 21)
- Our adoption as sons, the redemption of our bodies (v 23)

11. What is the thing that we are missing now, and that we hope for? (See also v 10.) How does this affect us at the moment (v 18, 23 and 26)? We are missing the redemption of our bodies, which is our adoption as sons of God (v 23). At present, with regard to the body, Christians are no different from non-Christians—our bodies are not yet redeemed. They remain the same as they were before we became Christians ie: weak, prone to sickness, dying. This is why v 10 tells us that for a Christian "your body is subject to death because of sin". Being stuck with unredeemed bodies means that for the present we suffer (v 18), we groan (v 23) and we are weak (v 26). Yet Christians are different—"The Spirit gives life because of righteousness" (v 10). Our spirits are alive because the Spirit lives in us, and that is the guarantee that our bodies will be redeemed and resurrected (Eph 1 v 12-14).

12. What does the Spirit do for us now, and how? He intercedes to God for us, because we are weak and do not know what we ought to pray for (v 26). The Spirit does this through wordless groans (v 26), and in accordance with God's will (v 27). This shows the amazing fellowship that the Spirit has with Christians—He lives with us in this frustrating, disappointing world that has set itself against God and His purposes, and He shares in the longing and groaning of God's people as we wait for the complete fulfilment of God's plans.

13. What is God's loving purpose for His children (v 28-30)? So what will the Spirit ask God on our behalf when He intercedes for us (v 27)? God's loving purpose for His children is that we will be conformed to the likeness of His Son (v 29). So when the Spirit intercedes for us in accordance with God's will (v 27), He asks God for whatever is required in a specific situation (and we probably don't know what that is) to make us more like Jesus.

14. APPLY: "We do not know what we ought to pray for." What does this mean? Remember that this is written in

the context of suffering (v 18). Compare
Philippians 1 v 21-24. In the context of
suffering we would all like to pray that God
would end our suffering, but that may not
be what we ought to pray for. Christians
may reach a point where they do not know
whether to pray for strength to continue
living in this world, or to ask God to take
them out of this world to be with Christ. So
Christians may have no idea how to pray,
even to the extent that they have no words
to utter, but they can be confident that the
Spirit will intercede to God for them, and
that He will do this completely in accordance
with God's will.

We know that God's great purpose for us is
to make us, and others around us, like His
Son, Jesus, but we don't know exactly what
is needed to achieve that. Philippians 1 v
21-24 is an example of a situation where it
is not easy to know what to pray for—Paul
wonders aloud whether it is better that he
continues to live in this world, or that he
goes to be with the Lord. Encourage your
group to think of other similar situations
eg: Should we stay in a difficult situation or
leave? Should we speak out or keep quiet?
In sickness, should we pray for healing,
endurance, or heaven?

• **Some people will say that, if God is
our Father, we will have perfect health
physically and emotionally. How can
this teaching bring us under a sense of
condemnation again?** Many Christians
mistakenly believe that they are suffering
ill-health and other problems in this world
because they do not have enough faith in
God. This leads them to doubt that God
loves them, and to spend all their time
searching out or confessing sins that they
think might have caused God to give up

on them. This takes their eyes off Jesus
and what He has done for them, and
causes them to turn to a false gospel of
works and obedience, in order to earn
God's love.

• **Why is this kind of teaching not only
wrong, but in opposition to the work
of the Spirit (v 22-25)?** It causes fear
and a sense of condemnation, which are
marks of the sinful nature, not the Spirit.
As we have seen in this passage, the Spirit
wants us to know that a life of suffering
is nothing less than the road to eternal life
for those who are no longer under any
condemnation because they are in Christ.
We should understand that groaning in
this present world is not an expression of
failure but of faith—it reveals our hope
and longing for the redeemed bodies that
our heavenly Father has promised.

15. APPLY What can separate you from the love of God in Christ Jesus? Nothing!

• **If you are "in Christ", what accusation
can anyone bring against you?**
Nothing! These verses were written to
people who were suffering persecution.
Because they followed Christ, they could
be accused of all sorts of things—breaking
the law, being bad citizens, dishonouring
their families etc. All of this can bring
us under a sense of condemnation.
Notice this comes out as a sense that
God no longer loves us and that He
wants to separate from us. It may be
helpful for your group to think about
what accusations from others bring them
under a sense of condemnation, and how
they should respond in the light of these
tremendous verses.

To see the full range of Good Book Guides, visit:
www.thegoodbook.co.uk (UK & Europe)
www.thegoodbook.com (US & Canada)